The First Software Patent and Other First Systems

Assist, the First Financial Commercial Language
CBM, the first Rational Bond Model

ANATOLY (TONY) KANDIEW

Order this book online at www.trafford.com
or email orders@trafford.com

Most Trafford titles are also available at major online book retailers.

Print information available on the last page.

ISBN: 978-1-4907-6254-8 (sc)
ISBN: 978-1-4907-6253-1 (e)

Trafford rev. 07/28/2015

North America & international
toll-free: 1 888 232 4444 (USA & Canada)
fax: 812 355 4082

Contents

Contents

The FIRST SOFTWARE PATENT and other FIRST SYSTEMS:
ASSIST, the First Financial Commercial Language
CBM, the First Rational Bond Model

Prologue

I joined Brookhaven National Laboratory in 1965. My friend from Control Data, Dan Kelly, helped me get the job. In fact he insisted that I talk to the Director of Applied Mathematics.

Dr. Y. Shimamoto had ordered a 6600 a while ago and it was being installed now. Dr. Shimamoto was also on the NASA evaluation team for the 1964 NASA RFP which awarded me the first prize for technical excellence for my solutions and timing analysis.

Dan wanted the best people at Brookhaven at that time, since the success or failure for the installation spelled serious money for him. A 6600 with all the peripheral gear at that time sold for about $10,000,000 dollars and his commission was 6%. So, you can understand how important that installation was for him.

Control Data paid the commission in 3 installments: First installment of 30% was paid at the time of the order. The second installment of 30% was paid after the installation, and the last installment of 40% was paid after the acceptance by the customer. Thus, at the time I joined Brookhaven, Dan had 70% of his commission outstanding.

In addition, he had received an "order of intent" for a second 6600 computer system and was negotiating an order for "EXTENDED CORE STORAGE", also a significant order.

In fact, Dan had pulled every string in Control Data to get the best installation team possible, because so much was riding for him for a smooth installation. And, that was one reason he wanted me at Brookhaven.

My interview was short and sweet. I got everything I asked for and was put to work right away. The first order of business was to augment the diagnostic facilities. Since I knew exactly what Control Data had available, I developed some "stress testing" diagnostics.

(My last few months at Control Data I spent at NYU trying to get serial number 4 accepted. After much grunt work and much sweat and many sleepless nights we got the 6600 accepted. So, I was well aware what was ahead. The only difference was that Brookhaven's 6600 was serial number 11 and was in much better shape when it was delivered. And, I was on the opposite team this time. But, we all had the same goal to make sure the 6600 was as clean and error free as possible).

This also exposed me to all departments in Applied Math. One of the key projects was to establish a "local network" and a more distant network. Sort of the start of the "INTERNET".

We wanted to connect all departments to our "super computer" and then connect to as many Universities as possible; such as Stony Brook, Ithaka, Albany, Buffalo and Rochester. The main problem we had was, we needed a "universal controller" which was not available in the "computer market."

Thus, our engineering group (in Applied Math) designed and started to build such a controller. A few months down the road our engineers were ready to test their first controller.

I lived in Wantagh, Long Island and across from me lived Niels Schumburg, an engineer in our engineering group and we commuted every day from Wantagh to Brookhaven, rain or shine; or snow or ice. On a good day the trip took us 1 hour and on a bad day it would take us up to 3 hours. So, we had plenty of time to talk about anything, and sometimes we talked about the "work related" problems.

When Niels started testing his first controller he would bombard me with all sorts of questions and I tried to give him an answer.

Niels needed machine time, initially once a week; then after a short time, twice a week and then every day. This became a real chore to Niels and to our Computing Facility.

The 6600 is a "super computer" it "digests" computing jobs at an incredible rate, executing instructions at the rate of 10 million instructions per second. Most jobs are "I/O" bound. That is, they read data from one medium and write or print data to another medium. These operations are very slow. They occur in the "MILLISECOND" range. That is, between one read or write operation, 10,000 computing operations can be performed (they can be issued at the rate of 100 nano seconds each).

Therefore, operators try to give the computer a good mix of jobs to maximize the computer utilization. With 7 partitions available, 7 different jobs are competing for the computer's resources. Thus, to give Niels 1 hour of dedicated machine time means the operators have to "idle down" the computer, which may take 2 to 3 hours.

When Niels was finished with his testing and turned the 6600 back to the operators, it may take 2 to 3 hours to "load up" the computer with the right job mix to get maximum utilization.

Therefore, one hour of dedicated machine time cost our facility roughly, on average, 6 hours (2.5+2.5+1.0). The going rate of the 6600 was about $3,000 dollars an hour. Thus, our daily cost was $18,000 dollars per day.

I heard it from all ends: From Niels how difficult it was to get machine time, and from the operators what a "pain in the neck" it was to give the machine to the engineers, and from accounting "the staggering cost of development."

We commuted for months arguing all the merits and demerits. Then, one day I told Niels: "What would you say if I wrote a program which would allow you to be on the machine all day long without crashing the system?"

Niels was flabbergasted. At first he did not believe it could be done. Then, as I convinced him that it could be done, he was ecstatic. He promised that all engineers and all operators would write a petition to Dr. Y. Shimamoto to ok this (my) project. With the "engineers in my pocket" I went that day to Yosh and told him about the project I was proposing.

His initial reaction was disbelief, but he did have much confidence in me (I had developed many useful diagnostics, I expanded and improved the compilers, FORTRAN in particular, and I produced a tape based UPDATE system which was very useful for very large programs, and I produced a SPY PROGRAM which produced a histogram of addresses and how frequently they were used by a program, thus allowing optimization. In particular for the four color problem).

The four color problem is a dozy. Every printer knows the solution (a printer needs only four colors to print any political map on our earth). But, for mathematicians that is not sufficient. A mathematician needs a proof. Thus, it was proven for every conceivable surface, except for a sphere, that four colors was all one needed. But, the proof for the sphere eluded to be proven. Dr. Y. Shimamoto (Yosh for short) had a particular attachment to that problem. He had solved it. But it was later found to have a flaw, and was discarded.

However, Yosh found a fellow in Germany, Heinrich Heesh who worked on the problem all his life. Heesh was trying to solve that problem by "enumeration;" using "Kempe Chains." Over the years he found a way of cataloging his solutions. All he needed was to find a "REDUCIBLE KEMPE CHAIN" and the problem was solved.

So, he started "manually." And, he catalogued each "irreducible Kempe Chain" on a piece of very thin, two inch square piece of paper. He catalogued them by the number of "Irreducible End Colorations."

Pretty soon he computed all tiny end coloration by hand. Then, being in a big University, he got machine time on a CDC 1604 and a PHD candidate to computerize the computations. But, by the time he got to the 14'ers he took all the machine time available on the University's computer system.

Heesh was able to convince Yosh that the solution was imminent "if he could only solve all the 14'ers. Thus, Yosh got him a grant to come to Brookhaven and solve his problem on our super computer.

Heinrich Heesh arrived at Brookhaven with two suitcases. One contained his belongings, and the other contained all his end colorations. His assistant was Karl Durre.

The next phase was to get them to use our super computer. So, Yosh assigned me to help Karl Durre to convert his program to our system. Within a few days the "show got on the road." Our operators loved that job. It was totally compute bound. It would crank away for one hour or so, and come up with a few numbers, and was done.

In no time at all we solved all the 14'ers, but the solution was not in sight. So, we went to the 15'ers and then to 16'ers. At that point our super computer would take 6 to 8 hours solving one 16'er.

So, I "spied" on the program and isolated the compute bound area. Then, I optimized the code and got roughly a 10 to 1 speed improvement. So, we finished the 16'ers and went to the 17'ers. When we reached the 18'ers we were back to the original problem.

By the time we reached the 19'ers, even Yosh began to realize that, that methodology was a "dead end" to be solved by "brute force." Thus, a disappointed Heinrich Heesh and Karl Durre returned home to Germany.

With the FOUR COLOR PROBLEM out of the way we continued with our CONTROLLER PROBLEM. Yosh brought together the BROOKNET engineers, our 6600 maintenance engineers, and our senior operations team and told me to present my idea to them while he listened and observed. The Brooknet engineers were all on my side and the Operations staff was on my side, but our maintenance engineers had some reservations. At the end of the meeting it was decided to bring a Control Data 6600 expert and then to repeat this meeting.

Yosh tried to get Seymour Cray but could not. (Goes to show you how important the project was in Yosh's eyes). Instead, Yosh was promised Thornton, the number 2 technician in Control Data from Arden Hill. When Thornton arrived our meeting was reconvened. I got the floor and started my presentation. (This time I was better prepared and identified all potential pitfalls).

Thornton listened patiently and then he replied: "It will not work." I challenged him for a specific case. He gave me a case and I showed him how my system would solve it dynamically. Still his answer was: "It will not work." So, I challenged him again. He gave me a new case, I solved it and he nixed it again. This went on for a while.

Then, Yosh tabled the meeting. Yosh took me into his office and gave me a promotion of sorts. I got a new title: BROOKNET COORDINATOR and I got a new office on the second floor (that's where all research fellows were) and I could pick a helper, an assistant (I picked Carl, a junior programmer) and best of all my project was ok'd.

My idea was simplicity itself. The 6600 is actually a computer which consists of 11 computers. One is the Central Processing Unit or CPU. It never stops. It runs all the time. It is surrounded by 10 Peripheral Processors or PPU's. The system monitor resides in a PPU and it has an instruction called EXCHANGE JUMP which can interrupt the CPU and directs it to begin execution from a new address (another program).

When a program in the CPU comes to an I/O operation it posts a CIO request and address in location 1 of its memory (60 bit word). The monitor reads location 1 of every partition and when it detects a CIO request or any other request in location 1 it springs into action. It stops the requestor and initiates a new program via the EXCHANGE JUMP.

Any PPU can communicate over any data channel. When a channel fails for any reason, the PPU servicing that channel hangs. If corrective action is not taken, other PPU's may be assigned to that channel and it too will hang. Thus eventually, the entire computing system freezes and the computer hangs.

I needed my monitor to be in a computer which never stopped (that is in the CPU) and had enough memory to maintain a series of tables. Thus, when my program began execution it requested a "ROVER type" PPU to keep track of every data channel.

It also maintained a table of each data channel. When it found one channel "potentially hanging" (that is in the same mode for 4 milliseconds or more) it would report back to the CPU and ask for corrective action. The CPU would analyze the request and then request that PPU to issue the "corrective" command, if needed. Then, the CPU would monitor that PPU. If the PPU responded, everything was "fixed on the fly" and the system was recovered. If the PPU did not respond for 10 milliseconds or more the CPU issued a request for another "Rover" and told him to time that channel for 10 milliseconds and then issue a corrective command. If the original PPU did not respond in the allotted time interval the second "ROVER" would issue the corrective command and thus release the first PPU and restore the channel. Notice, the monitor in the CPU had as many as 8 "ROVERS" or levels of corrective action. (I have never seen more than 2 to correct any channel failure).

Then I developed a language to make it easy for the engineers to program their device. When everything was finished, Niels and I tested the system. Once my system was operational it was called QUEST or "Quick Unprecedented Equipment Status Test."

Ever since then, our engineers had a field day. They could work all day and all night debugging their hardware without any degradation to the CENTRAL COMPUTING FACILITY.

Of course Yosh was extremely happy. He called Thornton and informed him that the project was completed and it allowed our engineers to debug their hardware online. Thornton did not believe him. He asked Yosh if he could send down his own engineers and stress test my system. Yosh agreed.

A few days later two "Field Engineers (FE's)" of Control Data Corporation arrived to test my system. We loaded my program and told them to go ahead. One of them turned to our operator and said: "Don't you need to take some preemptive action? Because I am going to crash your system!" Our operator just looked at him and replied: "No, you will not!"

Then, one FE walked up to a controller, took out a screw driver and began disabling the controller. While one FE worked on the controller, the other FE kept looking at the system monitor.

He saw a quick flash, when one "Rover" was hung. But in the next flash it was working again. So, now they changed positions. One disabled some logic boards while the other watched the monitor and again the same thing happened. One quick flash and they could see one PPU hang, but in the next flash the PPU was restored and the channel was cleared.

Then, they turned to me and said: "This is unbelievable!" After that they called Arden Hills, presumably they talked to Thornton. Well, that same day Thornton called Yosh and told him he wanted to buy that system. Yosh negotiated $1 Million dollars for my system in equipment for the Applied Math Department. Thus, my software was sold "AS IS" to Control Data.

> The minimum value of my system to Brookhaven was:
> $1,000,000 in hardware for the system from Control Data.
> $3,000*5*6*4.3*12 or $3,672,000 for engineering (minimum).
> (cost of machine time for 1 hour)* days in week * daily
> time to free one hour of stand alone machine time * number
> of weeks in a month * number of months in a year (minimum))

Thus, the machine time saved for the controller development group alone was, a minimum of $3,672,000 for one year. The engineering project lasted well over 10 years. Thus, the total savings to Brookhaven Lab was more than $30 million and an uncountable savings of time hours!

Once Yosh realized the value of my system commercially to Control Data, he urged me to patent it.

It should be noted that at that time the US Patent Office refused to issue any patents for SOFTWARE. Software was considered to be an IDEA and IDEAS were not patentable. Thus, Yosh recruited Brookhaven's LEGAL team to help me write up the patent.

At that time, a few departments in Brookhaven received patents. The one mentioned foremost was "El Dopa," which also received a Nobel Prize. However, Applied Math did not have a patent or a Nobel Prize.

(Of course there is no Nobel Prize for mathematics because of a personal vendetta between Nobel and a mathematician who eloped with Nobel's wife. In this way Nobel wanted to punish all future mathematicians forever).

So, I wrote up the patent description and submitted it to our legal team who submitted it to the US Patent Office on October 14, 1970.

Within a few weeks I received a letter and two documents from the US Patent Office. It requested for me to describe how my patent application was different from the description in the two documents.

Thus, I had to show why my patent application worked and the two papers had nothing to do with my invention. In other words, I had to defend my claim, against other claims. And, this process continued for two years!!!

In the end my patent was granted and became the first software patent ever granted by the US Patent Office. When it was granted, the engineering department and I had a major party at Niels's home. It was granted September 19, 1972; US 3,692,989. Since then, great many software patents were granted provided they used my "methodology" for patenting.

Once the two 6600's and the ECS storage were accepted by Brookhaven, Dan Kelly was seeking "greener pastures." Of course, as top salesman for Control Data he and his wife were wined and dined and were taken on a "world tour" by Control Data. When he returned he fell back on his friends Bill Stern and Penny Kaniclides. Penny was well connected and "rumors" had it that she controlled well over 30 million between her family and close friends.

Dan and I were with Control Data, when Control Data acquired Bendix. All entry level personnel left when Bendix's computer division was acquired, only senior programmers and managers were left for Control Data to digest. With their seniority from Bendix they "outranked" us all at Control Data, at east in New York. The new sales manager from Bendix assigned territory in accordance with the Telephone book directory. Most salespeople were mad as hell.

Penny started out as a Senior Programmer at Control Data and started learning the 1604. But, this did not suit her. So, she quit and joined Standard and Poor, a financial firm on Wall Street. She advanced rapidly at Standard and Poor and became Senior VP (she controlled substantial funds and that goes a long way in a financial firm).

At that time she inherited a project Standard and Poor was working on: To develop a financial language called FYNAL. A team of 8 people worked on that project for the last 5 years (40 man years) when Penny took control. She could clearly see that the project was not going anywhere and needed massive time, talent and resources.

So, one day she "accidentally" dropped a huge program (a few card cases full of punched cards) on the floor and resigned her job. She decided to form a financial company called TELSTAT. She took Bill Stern with her and a few other people.

Then, she turned to Dan Kelly to become her Sales Manager. And, Dan started working on me to come and join them to develop that "elusive" financial language which would "revolutionalize" the financial industry.

Somehow Yosh got wind of, that Dan was working on me to leave and join Telstat. But, he was determined to keep me. So, Yosh and I started to have lunches and outings and such things. All this time questioning me how my patent application was coming along.

I kept telling him how frustrating it was to have to defend my patent application with papers from IBM and AT&T for the most part, which had nothing to do with "fail safety." Well, each time I complained he had always an encouraging word. In the end he would say: "You get this patented, I will get you the Nobel Prize."

The trouble with his statement was that the Nobel Prize committee did not have a category for software, since this would be the first of its kind.

Of course, I listened to him and believed him until this kept on dragging out "forever." Meanwhile, the US Patent Office would send me two new documents to defend against.

This period of indecision, ended up costing me a "whole lot" in real dollars.

ASSIST

The financial commercial language posed a real challenge. But the key players of Telstat had the confidence in me that I could bring in that project in a reasonable time frame. Dan had told them about my NASA involvement, my work on the FOUR COLOR PROBLEM at Brookhaven and my PATENT application.

The money they offered was very good. In addition they offered to give me some stock. (Dan got 300,000 shares as I later found out). Bill got at least 3 times as much and Penny about 10 times as much. I was allowed to continue my patent defense and I was allowed to sign a consultant agreement with Brookhaven.

In order to bring in some money Penny hired a few high powered salesmen who approached people like Sorensen from PBS and many others. When I started negotiations, Telstat stock had not been sold yet. So, as far as the IRS was concerned the stock had no value. But, as I procrastinated because of Yosh, over 2,000,000 shares had been sold at $2.40 a share. This meant that if I was given any stock it would be treated as income. And, if I waited long enough I would not be able to take much stock at all, because the tax liability would "kill" me.

So, I made up my mind and joined Telstat. On the Telstat side they allowed me to continue my defense for the patent and on the Brookhaven side, Yosh gave me a maintenance contract for Quest (the existing system).

When I joined Telstat our contracted facilities were not yet ready. So, Penny rented a few rooms in the "Diplomat Hotel" on Park Avenue and 36th Street. It was a short distance to the 34th Street Train Terminal and I became a "Long Island Commuter." Soon, I found ways to make it to the train station without any exposure to the rain or snow.

The hotel was very convenient. It also provided free coffee, rolls with butter and pastry. But, it was also the hangout of some local hookers who tried to solicit business from us.

Our stay in that hotel was not very long. Then, we moved next to Bloomingdale's to our new and permanent address. This was actually much better for me. I could exit my train at Woodside Subway station and take the RR Subway to Bloomingdale's. My door to door commute was less than 1 hour.

My Patent correspondence kept right on going. I would get two papers to defend against. I would write my response and forward it to the Brookhaven legal department. They would put it into "legalese" and submit it to the US Patent office. It seemed as though I would be an old man with a long beard before my Patent was granted. I also stayed in touch with Yosh.

Yosh was an opera lover, and so was I. So, we spent many occasions to go to the opera together. Quite often when we went together to the opera he would reassure me that he would get the Nobel prize for me as soon as I would get my patent.

Meanwhile, I started developing the financial language. My biggest problem was, I did not know the financial terminology. Items like PE (price earnings ratio), HPRL and HPRH (holding period return, low and high, one of the more important analytical tools for stock selection), MVA (weighted moving averages) and so on.

Then, there were the various DOW theories, for each index, and the various indices with respect to one another and so on.

In addition, Telstat was constructing consolidated exchange trade data such as: HPRC (high price), LPRC (low price), CPRC (closing price), VOL (volume). The problem being that the price information existed on many databases: Daily, Weekly, Monthly, Quarterly, Semiannual, Annual and Compudat (S&P's proprietary database which Telstat subscribed to for a monthly fee). Thus, you can clearly see that "data addessabilty" would be the major stumbling block in any financial language.

Then, Telstat hired a financial analyst to develop many standard financial formula. Thus, the language needed to be subdivided between the PUBLIC DOMAIN and the PRIVATE DOMAIN allowing each to "crosstalk" to one another. Then, the entities we needed were:

Expressions or formulas which included elements from
the Private or Public domain. That is, entities connected
with operators (algebraic or logical).
(private) Items or user defined entities.
Criterions, expressions which yielded true or false results.
Groups, a list of TICKER SYMBOLS.
Composites or a mix of Ticker Symbols, Indexes and
groups.

Of course what was needed was a command which "Operated" on
them such as: DEFINE and REDEFINE. These commands allowed you
to define or change an entity.

The TIME subscript defined uniquely the database the entity resided
on. Thus, any "location" ambiguity was resolved that way.

Then, what was needed was a few "super utilities" and the language
was complete. They included:

PRINT	which included a number of clauses, such as: Company, Item, Period, Relative, Index and Type.
	The Type clause specified one of the 6 print permutations: Company / Time / Item expressed as CTI.
	(In this case it meant by COMPANY, Time Period across and Item down).
SELECT	Find a company subject to a certain expression or criterion.
SORT	Sort groups or indexes according to, up to three criteria or expressions.
RANK	Rank a group or index according to, up to three criteria or expressions.

Finally, a few 'Housekeeping commands" were in order.

COMMENT	Signifies user comment.
ECHO/NOECHO	Playback if desired.
EXPLAIN	Explains an entity.
DELETE	Deletes a private entity.
DESCRIBE	Describe usage of an entity or command.
END	Terminates program or session.
LIST	List an entity, such as group or expression.
ON/OFF	Prints summary of all errors.
PAGE and LINE	Set page and line number for a report.
USE	Establishes primary database.
WIDE	Invokes wide carriage (132 characters).

Then, of course, the primary "Universe" of usable databases was defined, the "language" definition was complete. And, once the language definition was complete, it became a cinch to write the language.

After about 6 months of development the language was complete and I started the "stress test mode." I expected to take 2 to 3 months to stress test every aspect. Penny and Bill were the greatest contributors to some "tricky" situation. Let me give you one example.

In the financial industry there are (were at that time) people who "sold companies" on the "sly." That is, they went around to other potential companies trying to sell a company or "testing the market" for potential sales. Usually they are small companies who wanted to find out if there was a market for a given company. They hired a "acquisition salesman" who then went around to various companies and played a "What if game."

That is, suppose he gave a few company characteristics and the potential acquisition price without disclosing the name of the company. This way he could "test the waters" for a potential sale. Well, to make a long story short, one day Penny received such a customer. As he was touting the attributes, Penny wrote them down; excused herself and came to me with the list of attributes. I wrote down the expression for these attributes and invoked the "SELECT" command. Within a few seconds out popped one company: US Nickel.

Then, I invoked the PRINT command and printed out all pertinent attributes for that company. An elated Penny took the printout back to the meeting and showed the results to the perplexed salesman. Such situations became quite frequent.

Within two months I stress tested all aspects of ASSIST and declared it ready for general use. That day all employee's of Telstat signed their name in the back of a preliminary USER MANUAL. (See signature page below).

ASSIST was ready just in time for a major financial conference and there the language made a huge "SPLASH." Every financial analyst wanted it and our sales people had a field day. They would not only sell ASSIST but many other "Consolidated Products."

Elaine Finger
Charlie Gessner
Frank Spano
Cheryl Natalor
Brenda Martin

Ron Lewis
Dale Sternlicht
Eric Dawson

Eric Kuchester

Michael Madej
Dave Simons
Pete Maggi

Joe Carvalheta
Roy Villanis
Tony Plaid

Janet Feller
Bill Stein
msily
Les Ussers

Kadn
Robyn Ray

Colleen Mc
Marie Gallagher

Joe Saunier
Herlesmann

Signature page of all the employee's
who wished me success of ASSIST.

CBM

Rational Corporate Bond Model

As soon as the ASSIST project was completed Penny and Bill identified another financial product which fit their company profile. They began specializing in "consolidated" tape deliveries. That is, many stocks may trade on many different exchanges: in New York, Philadelphia, Chicago and so on. Most financial reports are run only with consolidated data.

Thus, every day when the last exchange closed, all trade data was consolidated and tapes were cut. Then, messengers of every conceivable transportation mode (car, motorcycle, bicycle, roller skates, runners and walkers plus taxi) would wait for their designated tape and take it to their customer. Many were located in the down town area of Manhattan, but others had to go by plane to their destination. Remember in those days, in the 1970's, the Internet was not yet around and the data was needed as soon as it became available.

A group at MIT was developing a "NON TAXABLE" bond model; that is for MUNICIPALS. It was much easier to develop than a Corporate model because there were so many more non taxable bonds. The more bonds there are, the more trades were available. Hence there was more trade data. Roughly speaking, there were over 10 million non taxable bonds, while on the Corporate side there were roughly 15,000 issues. Thus, the Municipal model was "DENSE" as far as the trade data was concerned, while the Corporate trade data was very sparse. (Later on I added the Canadian Corporate bonds which contributed about 10,000 additional issues).

In the Municipal model the pricing strategy was entirely different from the model I developed. To deliver a pricing tape for 10 million issues was just not practical. Thus, the boys at MIT developed a BASE

MODEL, and "reversed the process." The subsequent price changes were recorded as a YIELD transformation. Then, using a SIMILARITY transformation the new yield were computed for the new model. Because, the original BASE Matrix was very dense, that process worked quite well. But, in order to price the desired bonds, the RATINGS needed to be updated. By developing such a pricing model one had to give up many desirable features. For example: The entire model was YIELD based and prices were derived from a YIELD to PRICE functional. Thus, it was difficult to incorporate a CALL SCHEDULE.

In addition, in my model one could use YIELD or PRICE as the basis. Then, when the RATING SURFACES were smoothed, it was sometimes easier to work with PRICES rather than YIELDS. And, last but not least, my model allowed the computation of RATIONAL QUALITIES, which the MIT model did not.

Because there were so few bonds that traded in the Corporate market, it was often difficult to form a well defined system to work with. Thus, in time (in the next phase) I developed a "MODEL LIBRARY."

The idea was actually quite simple. Once a model was "well defined" (and it passed all stabilization criteria such as: SMOOTHNESS, CONTINUITY and COMPLETENESS" it could be characterized by its "TREASURY YIELD CURVE." That is, the curvature could be expressed as a "FUNCTIONAL" and stored in the library with the entire model. Then, when the market was very erratic, a "FUNCTIONAL" could be constructed with the present Treasury Yield Curve. Then, the library could be searched for the best fitting model on that library. That model had all the desired characteristics and could be used for pricing in a very erratic market.

In addition, it was prudent to subdivide the model into the many sectors with very similar characteristics. For example the Government bonds included also all its AGENCIES. And, the Corporate Bonds, I subdivided into 10 major industries such as: Telephones, Utilities, Industrials and so on.

Consider the primary attributes of the MODEL: Time to Maturity, Coupon, and Quality. They formed the basis of a 3 dimensional space. But, because the Time to Maturity could span a very long interval (0 to 30 years) it needed to be subdivided into manageable sub intervals. I chose four intervals:

1) 0 to 2 years
2) 2 to 5 years
3) 5 to 10 years and
4) 10 to 30 years.

I called the time interval of 2, 5 and 10 years the transition zones. This is where one zone abuts to the next zone. Thus, in the data selection process each zone was limited to a fixed number of trades (so that no zone would overpower the results), while the transition zones ranging from 1 to 3 years, 4 to 6 years, and 9 to 11 years would accept twice the number of trades. This way no single zone would overpower the model. And, in this way the transition from one zone to another would be much smoother.

Of course, the most important corporate bonds, or "TAXABLE BONDS" are the TREASURY BONDS. Even though they are called by different names when they mature at different times (they could be called BILLS, NOTES or BONDS), together they form the TREASURY YIELD CURVE. The treasury yield curve is that curve which shows the yield at a "Par Price" of 100% or simply 100. However, in real life, for pricing purposes, the curve is not a simple curve, but a SURFACE, where the treasury yield curve separates the PREMIUM MARKET from the DISCOUNT MARKET on that pricing surface. The other directions are: QUALITY and COUPON.

You can look at QUALITY as a "mechanism" which stacks the many QUALITY surfaces and the COUPON spans the underlying surface.

Once you understand the "TREASURIES" the remaining corporates are very similar. They form a surface (along the coupon axis) for each QUALITY. Thus, a complete corporate bond model has surfaces for all (MOODY QUALITY RATINGS), none of which may intersect. Then, when we look at YIELD to MATURITY they must behave in the following manner:

YIELDS: TREASURIES< AAA < AA < A < BAA < BA < B < C < D

and

PRICE: TREASURIES> AAA > AA > A > BAA > BA > B > C > D

Note, Yield to Maturity consists of 1) Current Yield which is Coupon divided by Price times 100, and 2) the appreciation of the bond to its redemption value, which is 100% or $1,000. Since all bonds trade at a denomination of $1,000. (Very few trade at a higher denomination).

Thus, you can readily see that PRICES and YIELDS are directly coupled and inversely related. That is, given a PRICE, then the YIELD for a given COUPON and MATURITY is determined. That is, there is a functional which couples both PRICE and YIELD. (Notice, QUALITY plays no role any longer). That is, PRICE and YIELD are directly coupled; while PRICE and QUALITY; and YIELD and QUALITY is LOOSELY coupled.

Then we can express this as a set of equations. If

q stands for Quality,

c stands for Coupon and

t stands for Time to Maturity and

Yield stands for Yield to Maturity, then we have:

PRICE = $H(q,c,t)$ and YIELD = $G(q,c,t)$; then there exist a function $R(c,t)$ which binds PRICE and YIELD. And,

PRICE = $R(c,t,yield)$ and YIELD = $R(c,t,price)$

Later on in the 1980's, the MOODY ratings were further subdivided into 1, 2, 3 subsets such as: AA1 < AA2 < AA3 for all investment grade rating classes: AA, A, BAA.

Let's for a moment go back to the MOODY scale. Notice the highest rated bond is actually not rated at all. That is, Government bonds are the STRONGEST bonds in the market! Look at it this way: IF the Government fails, ALL BONDS WILL FAIL.

Then, what do the ratings mean? According to MOODY'S they measure the RISK OF DEFAULT. Thus the ratings AAA to BAA are called INVESTMENT GRADE bonds. All bonds below the rating of BAA are called JUNK BONDS. A "D" rating means the bond is in default. (During the time I was building the model MICHAEL MILKEN was the JUNK BOND KING. And, we had to make all kinds of deals with him to get his trade data. He sold it dearly to us, but it proved to be worth while).

A well behaved model should also give you the opportunity to compute a RATING. But, notice these ratings are dynamic, market defined ratings. Not some guesswork of accountants. (As you can see I am a believer in automated systems whenever possible).

That is, there is a functional: Quality = K1(c,t, Price) and another functional: Quality = K2(c,t, YIELD). Thus, the dynamic quality produced by the model is much more significant, and varies much more than the static Moody ratings. Unfortunately it takes a "massive crash" before my statement is verified. Therefore, the debacle of 2008, could have been avoided had my model been in widespread use!

In addition to the main variables of q,c,t there are additional variables which come into play when their influence becomes important. Let me discuss only two. All Bonds are issued with a list of PROVISIONS. All Bonds have a provision called SINKING FUND and CALL SCHEDULE. That is, all bonds except for the GOVERNMENT BONDS.

Let's discuss the SINKING FUND provision first. When you buy a Corporate bond, you are buying a Corporate obligation. All the provisions are listed in the bond document (contract). The company promises to pay the stated coupon value annually in two semi annual installments.

The Sinking Fund provision states that over time, the company will buy back a small percentage of its bonds outstanding, say 3% each year. Then, if it is a 30 year bond to begin with, at maturity there would only be 10% outstanding. In theory this is fine. But, in practice here's what happens.

Initially, the company has no problem in buying back the required number of bonds. But, as time goes on, it becomes harder and harder to obtain the bonds. This is done deliberately by the investors. Thus, for the company to buy back its bonds it offers a premium! This process is called "SQUEEZING THE SINKER." This premium can reach occasionally as much as 2%, or $2 for every $100.

Next, let's talk about the CALL PROVISION. The idea is as follows. Given a market where the interest rates decline; then, the company would like to call in some outstanding bonds and reissue them at a lower rate (lower coupon), thus saving money in the process! Well, that is essentially what call provisions do. But, to make the bonds attractive to a buyer, a "CALL PROTECTION" is build into the call schedule. Normally it is

5 years. Thus, when the market yields are "sky high" the bond buyer is protected for 5 years to receive maximum yields, but in the 6th year the call schedule takes effect. Thus, when the rational market price is above the CALL PRICE the company is very likely to call that bond. Therefore, the bond must be priced accordingly, at most $1 above the specific (c,t) call schedule price.

So, why do the Government bonds do not have any provisions? Well, "it is said that" the US Government issues so many bonds and chooses so many brokerage houses to sell these bonds that it would be inundated by the additional paper work.

Another factor which may play havoc in a pricing model (hence yield model) is the VOLUME. Small investors may buy one or two bonds at a time. But, INSTITUTIONAL investors buy one million, or two million in bonds at a time. Thus, institutional investors may get a DISCOUNT of up to $2 per $100 or $20 per $1,000. Keep in mind that the NORMAL denomination of a bond is in $1,000 dollars. Thus, I made my model to reflect the INSTITUTIONAL investor at $1,000,000 dollars.

Once the basic model characteristics were in place all that remained was to define the model facilities. They included an extensive Print module, a number of "SUPER UTILITIES" and a number of maintenance and control functions. (A partial report sample is included). Then we have:

PRINT	Print facilities, see sample attached.
AMORTIZATION	Given an Amount, an interest rate, a time to maturity and payment frequency (Weekly, Biweekly, Juppy, Monthly, Quarterly, Annual) and compute the amortization schedule).
CUSIP	Phonetic name to Cusip search. Given a name (even one which is misspelled) list the entities who match the PHONETIC search, providing CUSIP NUMBER).

DEDICATION	Given a PORTFOLIO of expected payments due, find the bonds in a point by point fashion to IMMUNIZE that PORTFOLIO.
FUTURE	Given 3 or 5 points on the TREASURY YIELD CURVE, go find the model on the MODEL LIBRARY which fits best these characteristics
IMMUNIZATION	Given a PORTFOLIO of expected payments due, find bonds which best (in the least square sense) IMMUNIZE that PORTFOLIO.
PERFORMANCE	Compute the UNIT VALUE of an INVESTMENT PORTFOLIO.
PRESENT VALUE	COMPUTE the Present Value.
SWAP	Given a Bond or Bond list and criteria, provide an optimized Target list and Substitute list with the Price and Tax consequences.

UTILITIES

ATTACH	Attach a file.
DESCRIBE	Describe a command.
DETACH	Detach a file.
EXPLAIN	Explain a command.
END	Terminate session, job or procedure.
LIST	List all commands.

As soon as I completed the BOND MODEL, I was granted the patent from the Patent Office: US PATENT # 3,692,989! My friend

Niels, his boss Arnold Peskin and I had a nice party. The big question was: What comes next. I was exhausted both physically and mentally. The biggest drain was the defense of the myriad of papers I had to fight which had very little to do with "FAIL SAFETY OF COMPUTERS."

Then I waited for YOSH. He called and we scheduled a night at the OPERA. We saw Wagner's WALKURE. This is when Yosh "hemmed and hawed" and explained to me that it will be impossible to get the NOBEL PRIZE. The Computer field was new and it was impossible to find a category where my Patent would qualify. Thus, all that procrastination at BROOKHAVEN cost me many shares of TELSTAT stock for nothing.

Finally, my friend DANIEL KELLY had disappeared. Actually, he disappeared just before I finished the ASSIST project. I asked BILL STERN, who was his good friend, but BILL knew "NOTHING." Then, out of the blue I got a call from DAN. He wanted to meet me at the GASLIGHT CLUB. So, I went to the Gaslight Club.

Dan was in a great mood and he was happy to see me. As soon as we got seated I asked him what happened. And, DAN unraveled his story.

To begin with, his son disappeared with his girlfriend. Both were minors and Dan hired immediately a detective. The detective located them in Boston and Dan immediately took off to Boston. But they got wind of his coming and fled. And, so began a six months chase until their money run out. Then, DAN was able to convince them to come home and do everything the normal way.

But, when Dan returned, Bill Stern and PENNY forced Dan to give up his stock (300,000 shares of TELSTAT stock) "because he abandoned the company at the most critical time." I felt that was a mean and vicious thing to do (since he responded to a family crisis as every father would do), and I felt threatened for the stock I held and the taxes I paid. This was also the first time I found out how much stock Dan held. This became my basis of discontent.

It so happened that I could exercise my stock at that time. Which I did. Then I found a buyer at Telstat who was willing to pay me $12 a share for my 3,000 shares. Rumors had it that PENNY was negotiating the sale of TELSTAT to WESTERN UNION at $24 a share, which took place a year later. Then, I quit Telstat and joined GENERAL REINSURANCE. I gave Penny the standard 2 weeks notice and offered to sign a consultants agreement just like the one I had with Yosh. But,

Penny refused to give me that consultant agreement. (Her experience at Standard and Poor taught her that consultants take the best jobs for the maximum pay and produce very little. A form of "JOB SECURITY.")

Thus, we parted company.

Sample Report Pages of CBM

ACCOUNT R2735 · 70 FIRST NATIONAL BANK COLLECT. INV. FUND B   3/31/83 CLIENT 001 PAGE 4

DISTRIBUTION OF BONDS BY MATURITIES - MARKET VALUE

MATURITY	COST	MARKET VALUE	% OF PORT.	% PORT. EX. CASH	EST. ANNUAL INCOME	CURR YIELD	YIELD TO MATU.
LESS THAN 1 YEAR - TAXABLE	0	0	.00	.00			
1 - 3 YEARS - TAXABLE	280,105	270,312	5.66	7.76	35,937	13.29	9.95
3 - 5 YEARS - TAXABLE	0	0	.00	.00			
5 - 10 YEARS - TAXABLE	744,843	812,187	16.99	23.31	103,437	12.74	12.14
10-15 YEARS - TAXABLE	0	0	.00	.00			
15-20 YEARS - TAXABLE	334,100	334,022	6.99	9.59	18,437	5.52	5.87
OVER 20 YEARS - TAXABLE	2,231,975	2,068,185	43.27	59.35	234,436	11.34	11.52
LESS THAN 1 YEAR - TAX-FREE	0	0	.00	.00			
1 - 3 YEARS - TAX-FREE	0	0	.00	.00			
3 - 5 YEARS - TAX-FREE	0	0	.00	.00			
5 - 10 YEARS - TAX-FREE	0	0	.00	.00			
10-15 YEARS - TAX-FREE	0	0	.00	.00			
15-20 YEARS - TAX-FREE	0	0	.00	.00			
OVER 20 YEARS - TAX-FREE	0	0	.00	.00			
TOTAL	3,591,023	3,484,706	72.91	100.00	392,247	11.26	11.00
CASH EQUIVALENTS	1,294,700	1,294,700	27.09		101,993	7.88	7.88
GRAND TOTAL	4,885,723	4,779,406	100.00		494,240	10.34	10.15

16

CLIENT 001

3/31/83   PAGE 2

ACCOUNT R2735 70 FIRST NATIONAL BANK COLLECT. INV. FUND B

PORTFOLIO HOLDINGS

QUANTITY	DESCRIPTION	UNIT COST	MARKET PRICE	TOTAL COST	MARKET VALUE	UNREAL. GAIN/LOSS	% OF TOTAL	CURR. YIELD	YTM
	UTILITY								
250,000	COLUMBUS & SOUTHERN OHIO ELEC 13.625% 10-1-90 A-3	99.87	109.38	249,687	273,437	23,750	5.7		11.71
250,000	PENNSYLVANIA PWR & LT 1ST MTG 14.% 12-01-1990 A-2	100	109	250,000	272,500	22,500	5.7		12.15
250,000	PHILADELPHIA ELECTRIC 1ST & REF 13.75% 10-15-92 A-2	98.06	106.50	245,156	266,250	21,094	5.6		12.56
250,000	DUKE POWER CO 1ST & REF MTG 7.375% 12-1-2002 BAA-3	66.41	66.38	166,015	165,937	-78	3.5		11.81
250,000	ILLINOIS POWER CO 1ST MTG 7.625% 6-1-2003 A-1	68.09	67.50	170,235	168,750	-1,485	3.5		11.91
300,000	CENTRAL ILLINOIS LT CO 1ST MTG 9.25% 3-1-2005 AA-3	80.45	79.50	241,341	238,500	-2,841	5.0		11.90
250,000	PUBLIC SERVICE CO INDIANA 1ST MTG 7.625% 1-1-2007 A-3	54.97	65.25	162,432	163,125	693	3.4		12.10
	TOTAL UTILITY			1,484,866	1,548,499	63,633	32.4		12.12
	INDUSTRIAL								
250,000	WEYERHAEUSER CO DEB 8.90% 11-15-2004 AA-3	90	79.75	225,000	199,375	-25,625	4.2		11.45
300,000	SEARS ROEBUCK & CO DEB REG 7.875% 2-1-2007 AA-2	99.75	71.50	299,250	214,500	-84,750	4.5		11.36
	TOTAL INDUSTRIAL			524,250	413,875	-110,375	8.7		11.08

ACCOUNT R2735 70 FIRST NATIONAL BANK COLLECT. INV. FUND B

CLIENT 001

3/31/83   PAGE 3

PORTFOLIO HOLDINGS

QUANTITY	DESCRIPTION	UNIT COST	MARKET PRICE	TOTAL COST	MARKET VALUE	UNREAL. GAIN/LOSS	% OF TOTAL	CURR. YIELD	YTM
	FINANCIAL								
150,000	CITICORP NOTES REG 10.875% 6-15-2010 AA-1	90.25	89.50	135,370	134,250	-1,120	2.8	12.21	12.15
	TOTAL FINANCIAL			135,370	134,250	-1,120	2.8	---	12.15
	OTHER								
168,085.780	MORTGAGES		100	168,085	168,085	0	3.5	11.26	---
	TOTAL OTHER			168,085	168,085	0	3.5	---	---
	TOTAL SENIOR SECURITIES			3,591,023	3,484,706	-106,317	72.9	11.26	
	TOTAL PORTFOLIO			4,885,723	4,779,406	-106,317	100.0	10.34	

18

ACCOUNT R2735 70 FIRST NATIONAL BANK COLLECT. INV. FUND B   3/31/83   PAGE 5   CLIENT 001

DISTRIBUTION OF BONDS BY TYPE

ISSUER TYPE	COST	MARKET VALUE	% OF PORT.	% PORT. EX. CASH	EST. ANNUAL INCOME	CURR YIELD	YIELD TO MATU.
U S GOVERNMENT	779,802	756,247	15.82	22.80	87,812	11.61	10.42
U S GOVERNMENT AGENCY	0	0	.00	.00			
U S MORTGAGE PASS THROUGH	0	0	.00	.00			
CONVENTIONAL PASS THROUGH	0	0	.00	.00			
TELEPHONE	498,650	463,750	9.70	13.98	54,500	11.75	11.76
UTILITY	1,464,866	1,548,499	32.40	46.69	187,748	12.12	12.04
INDUSTRIAL	524,250	413,875	8.66	12.48	45,875	11.08	11.40
FINANCIAL	135,370	134,250	2.81	4.05	16,312	12.15	12.21
TRANSPORTATION	0	0	.00	.00			
FOREIGN	0	0	.00	.00			
TOTAL	3,422,938	3,316,621	69.39	100.00	392,247	11.83	11.56
CASH EQUIVALENTS	1,294,700	1,294,700	27.09		101,993	7.88	7.88
GRAND TOTAL	4,885,723	4,779,406	100.00		494,240	10.34	10.52

302

ACCOUNT R2735 70 FIRST NATIONAL BANK COLLECT. INV. FUND B   3/31/83   PAGE   6

DISTRIBUTION OF BONDS BY COUPON VALUE

COUPON	COST	MARKET VALUE	% OF PORT.	% PORT. EX. CASH	EST. ANNUAL INCOME	CURR YIELD	YIELD TO MATU.
LESS THAN 5.00%	168,085	168,085	3.52	4.82			
5.00 TO 7.99%	797,932	712,312	14.90	20.44	80,186	11.26	11.76
8.00 TO 10.99%	1,600,058	1,521,810	31.84	43.67	172,687	11.35	11.44
11.00 TO 13.99%	494,843	539,687	11.29	15.49	68,437	12.68	12.13
MORE THAN 14.0%	530,105	542,812	11.36	15.58	70,937	13.07	11.05
TOTAL	3,591,023	3,484,706	72.91	100.00	392,247	11.26	11.00
CASH EQUIVALENTS	1,294,700	1,294,700	27.09		101,993	7.88	7.88
GRAND TOTAL	4,885,723	4,779,406	100.00		494,240	10.34	10.15

ACCOUNT   R2735   70   FIRST NATIONAL BANK COLLECT. INV. FUND B   3/31/83   PAGE   7

BOND AND CASH EQUIVALENT CHARACTERISTICS REPORT

	TOTALS	U S GO	U S GO	U S MO	CONVEN	TELEPH	UTILIT	INDUST	FINANC	TRANSP
EXCLUDED CASH EQUIVAL										
AVERAGE MATURITY	20.3	19.8	0.0	0.0	0.0	36.7	14.5	22.8	27.2	0.0
AVERAGE COUPON	10.9	11.8	0.0	0.0	0.0	10.9	11.1	8.4	10.9	0.0
AVERAGE QUALITY	80.1	100.0	0.0	0.0	0.0	60.0	71.3	75.2	90.0	0.0
AVR MKT DURATION	7.4	6.7	0.0	0.0	0.0	8.9	6.9	8.9	8.4	0.0
AVR PAR DURATION	7.7	6.9	0.0	0.0	0.0	8.9	7.2	8.9	8.4	0.0
INCLUDED CASH EQUIVAL										
AVERAGE MATURITY	14.6									
AVERAGE COUPON	10.0									
AVERAGE QUALITY	87.2									
AVR MKT DURATION	5.4									
AVR PAR DURATION	5.7									

ACCOUNT   R6601   70   SEAFARERS PENSION PLAN - INVESTED INCOME ACCOUNT

CLIENT 00\
3/31/83   PAGE   2

1   1
5   4
1

DISTRIBUTION OF BONDS BY MATURITIES - MARKET VALUE

MATURITY	COST	MARKET VALUE	% OF PORT.	% PORT. EX. CASH	EST. ANNUAL INCOME	CURR YIELD	YIELD TO MATU.
LESS THAN 1 YEAR - TAXABLE	0	0	.00	.00			
1 - 3 YEARS - TAXABLE	0	0	.00	.00			
3 - 5 YEARS - TAXABLE	0	0	.00	.00			
5 -10 YEARS - TAXABLE	375,000	386,250	10.43	100.00	30,000	7.77	11.58
10-15 YEARS - TAXABLE	0	0	.00	.00			
15-20 YEARS - TAXABLE	0	0	.00	.00			
OVER 20 YEARS - TAXABLE	0	0	.00	.00			
LESS THAN 1 YEAR - TAX-FREE	0	0	.00	.00			
1 - 3 YEARS - TAX-FREE	0	0	.00	.00			
3 - 5 YEARS - TAX-FREE	0	0	.00	.00			
5 -10 YEARS - TAX-FREE	0	0	.00	.00			
10-15 YEARS - TAX-FREE	0	0	.00	.00			
15-20 YEARS - TAX-FREE	0	0	.00	.00			
OVER 20 YEARS - TAX-FREE	0	0	.00	.00			
TOTAL	375,000	386,250	10.43	100.00	30,000	7.77	11.58
CASH EQUIVALENTS	3,316,328	3,316,328	89.57		287,025	8.65	8.65
GRAND TOTAL	3,691,328	3,702,578	100.00		317,025	8.56	8.96

22

ACCOUNT R2735 70 FIRST NATIONAL BANK COLLECT. INV. FUND B .... 3/31/83   CLIENT 001 PAGE 1

PORTFOLIO HOLDINGS

QUANTITY	DESCRIPTION	UNIT COST	MARKET PRICE	TOTAL COST	MARKET VALUE	UNREAL. GAIN/LOSS	% OF TOTAL	CURR. YIELD	YTM
	LIQUID RESERVES								
	CASH & EQUIVALENTS								
	CASH			-1,040,150	-1,040,150	0	21.8-	---	8.00
800,000	U S TREASURY BILLS DUE 5/26/83	98.11		784,881	784,881	0	16.4	---	7.97
500,000	U S TREASURY BILLS DUE 6/ 9/83	97.92		489,610	489,610	0	10.2	---	8.40
1,060,359	U S GOVT SEC SHORT TERM FD	100	100	1,060,359	1,060,359	---	22.2	---	7.69
	TOTAL CASH & EQUIVALENTS			1,294,700	1,294,700	0	27.1	---	7.88
	TOTAL LIQUID RESERVES			1,294,700	1,294,700	0	27.1	---	7.88
	SENIOR SECURITIES								
	U S GOVERNMENT								
250,000	U S TREASURY NOTE 14.375% 5-15-85 AAA	112.04	108.13	280,105	270,312	-9,793	5.7	---	9.95
500,000	U S TREASURY BOND 10.375% 11-15-2012 AAA	95.94	97.19	499,697	485,935	-13,762	10.2	---	10.69
	TOTAL U S GOVERNMENT			779,802	756,247	-23,555	15.8	---	11.61
	TELEPHONE								
500,000	SOUTHERN BELL TEL CO 10.90% 12-1-2019 A-1	99.73	92.75	498,650	463,750	-34,900	9.7	---	11.76
	TOTAL TELEPHONE			498,650	463,750	-34,900	9.7	---	11.75

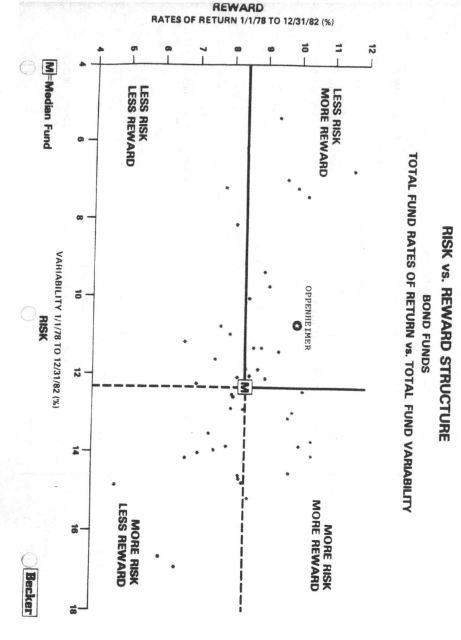

RISK vs. REWARD STRUCTURE
BOND FUNDS
TOTAL FUND RATES OF RETURN vs. TOTAL FUND VARIABILITY

REWARD
RATES OF RETURN 1/1/78 TO 12/31/82 (%)

VARIABILITY 1/1/78 TO 12/31/82 (%)
RISK

LESS RISK
LESS REWARD

LESS RISK
MORE REWARD

MORE RISK
MORE REWARD

MORE RISK
LESS REWARD

OPPENHEIMER

M = Median Fund

Becker

First Software Patent granted by the U.S. Patent Office

United States Patent
Kandiew

[15] **3,692,989**
[45] **Sept. 19, 1972**

[54] **COMPUTER DIAGNOSTIC WITH INHERENT FAIL-SAFETY**

[72] Inventor: **Anatoly I. Kandiew,** Wantagh, N.Y.

[73] Assignee: **The United States of America as represented by the United States Atomic Energy Commission**

[22] Filed: **Oct. 14, 1970**

[21] Appl. No.: **80,651**

[52] U.S. Cl. 235/153, 340/172.5
[51] Int. Cl. G06f 11/00
[58] Field of Search 235/153; 340/146.1, 172.5

[56] **References Cited**

UNITED STATES PATENTS

3,387,276	6/1968	Reichow	340/172.5
3,348,197	10/1967	Akers, Jr. et al.	235/153 X
3,377,623	4/1968	Reut et al.	340/172.5
3,409,877	11/1968	Alterman et al.	340/172.5
3,451,042	6/1969	Jensen et al.	340/146.1 X
3,510,845	5/1970	Couleur et al.	340/172.5
3,517,171	6/1970	Avizienis	235/153
3,519,808	7/1970	Lawder	235/153

OTHER PUBLICATIONS

Downing et al., No. 1 ESS Maintenance Plan, The Bell System Technical Journal, September 1964, pp. 1961–2019.

Primary Examiner—Charles E. Atkinson
Attorney—Roland A. Anderson

[57] **ABSTRACT**

Time-saving, effective and efficient diagnostic means and method for the Brooknet shared time computer system for fail-safe operation on a regular job priority basis while the computer system is operating to handle other jobs and without dedicating the entire computer system to the diagnostic function.

10 Claims, 10 Drawing Figures

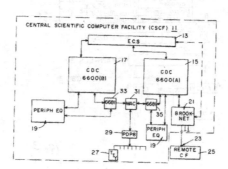

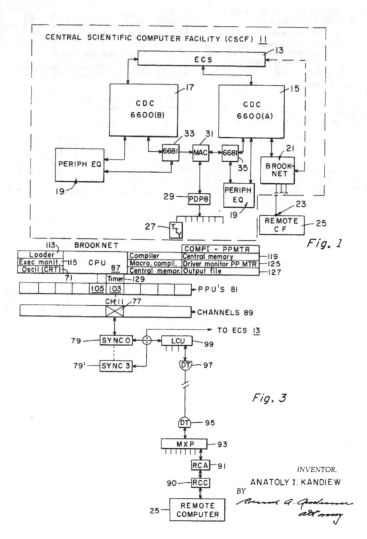

PATENTED SEP 19 1972
3,692,989
SHEET 1 OF 4
CENTRAL SCIENTIFIC COMPUTER FACILITY (CSCF) 11
ECS
13
CDC 6600(B)
17
CDC 6600(A)
15
33
31
6681
MAC
6681
21
PERIPH EQ
35
BROOK-NET
19
29
PDP8
PERIPH EQ
23
19
27
TTY
REMOTE CF
25
Fig. 1
113
BROOKNET
COMPI - PPMTR
Loader
Compiler
Central memory
119
Exec monit.
115
CPU
Macro. compil.
Driver monitor PP MTR
125
Oscil (CRT)
87
Central memor.
Output file
127
71
Timer
129
105
103
PPU'S 81
CH 11
77
CHANNELS 89
TO ECS 13
79
SYNC 0
LCU
99
79'
SYNC 3
DT
97
Fig. 3
DT
95
MXP
93
RCA
91
INVENTOR.
90
RCC
ANATOLY I. KANDIEW
BY
25
REMOTE COMPUTER

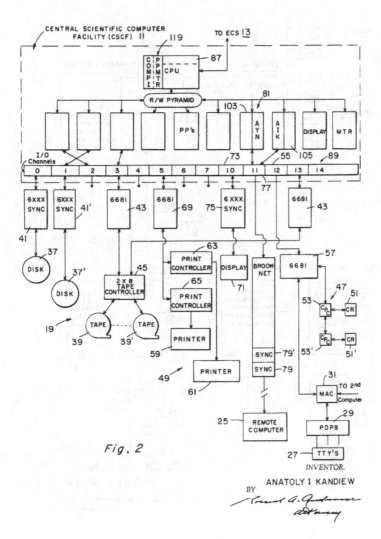

Fig. 2

INVENTOR.
ANATOLY I KANDIEW
BY

PATENTED SEP 19 1972
3,692,989
SHEET 3 OF 4
CHANNEL I
77
FP
F/E
A/I
DATA
DATA
DATA
DATA
PPU COMMAND
DEVICE
DEVICE EG. {SYNCRONIZERS 6681-79}
RESPOND TO PPU COMMAND
25
Fig. 4
CASE A: PPU COMMAND = "FUNCTION"
103
FP=1 FULL ACTIVE
DATA
PPU 103
DEVICE RECEIVE FUNCTION PROPEGATE TO PROPER UNIT AND REPLY
25
FP=0 EMPTY INACTIVE
DATA
PPU 103
Fig. 5
CASE B INPUT INTO "A" (1 WORD INPUT)
FP=0 EMPTY ACTIVE
NO DATA
PPU 103
DEVICE DETECTING(E,A, FP=0) NOW SHOULD SEND DATA WORD
25
FP=0 FULL ACTIVE
DATA
PPU 103
Fig. 6a
CASE C: (1 WORD OUTPUT)
FP=0 FULL ACTIVE
DATA
PPU 103
DEVICE ACKNOLEDGES ACCEPTANCE OF DATA BY REPLYING
25
FP=0 EMPTY ACTIVE
NO DATA
PPU 103
Fig. 6b
INVENTOR.
ANATOLY I KANDIEW
BY

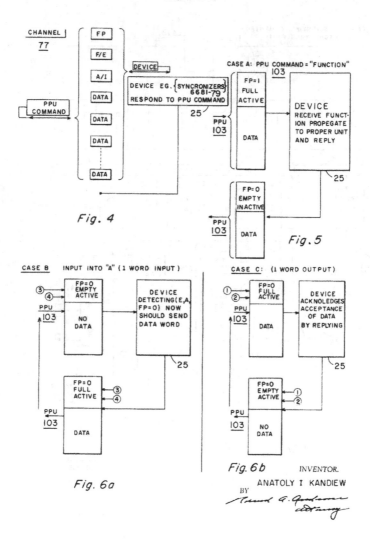

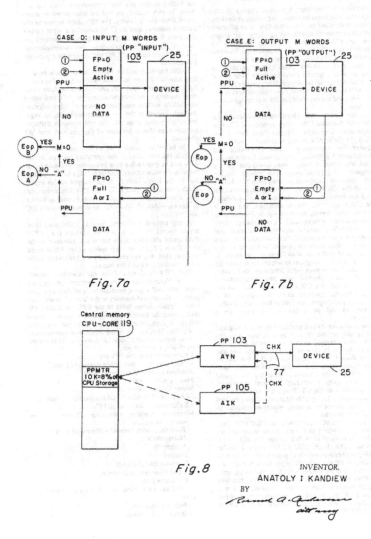

PATENTED SEP 19 1972
3,692,989
SHEET 4 OF 4
CASE D: INPUT M WORDS
(PP "INPUT")
103
25
FP=0
Empty
Active
PPU
DEVICE
NO
DATA
NO
YES
Eop B
M=0
YES
Eop A
NO
"A"
FP=0
Full
A or I
PPU
DATA
Fig. 7a
CASE E: OUTPUT M WORDS
(PP "OUTPUT")
103
25
FP=0
Full
Active
PPU
DEVICE
NO
DATA
YES
M=0
Eop
YES
NO
"A"
Eop
FP=0
Empty
A or I
PPU
NO
DATA
Fig. 7b
Central memory
CPU-CORE 119
PPMTR
10 K=8% of
CPU Storage
PP 103
AYN
CHX
DEVICE
25
77
CHX
PP 105
AIK
Fig. 8
INVENTOR.
ANATOLY I KANDIEW
BY
att'y

3,692,989

1

COMPUTER DIAGNOSTIC WITH INHERENT FAIL-SAFETY

BACKGROUND OF THE INVENTION

In the field of computers, it is advantageous to connect central computers to remote input-output devices, such as remote input-output computers, in an effective shared time computer system having a large, fast-acting central scientific computing facility, referred to hereinafter as a CSCF. At the Brookhaven National Laboratory, for example, there are many groups that have their own relatively small computers that are located at widely spaced distances from their CSCF and it is advantageous to connect these remote computers as well as other remote input-output devices to the CSCF to expand the capability of the remote input-output devices.

Examples of such remote input-output devices at the Brookhaven National Laboratory comprise a Chemistry Department Computer, a Physics Department Computer, a 33 GeV Alternating Gradient Synchrotron Computer for experimental data processing and machine control, a Medical Department Computer, an Applied Mathematics Department Computer for the investigation of graphic displays of crystals, etc., a remote computer for communicating back FOCUS for forth with the CSCF for implementing a system called FOCUS for providing on-line file handling capabilities to the CSCF users via remote teletypes, and a wide variety of other remote input-output devices at locations up to a mile or more apart for monitoring experiments, controlling special equipment, storing and processing a wide variety of data, accumulating data from many widely spaced locations, and performing a wide variety of arithmetical and logical operations. In this regard, it is advantageous to selectively expand the capabilities of any remote input-output device by functional integration thereof with the computational power and speed of a CSCF, but heretofore this has required difficult, expensive, and time-consuming trouble-shooting and diagnostics, and/or has involved other problems, as will be understood in more detail hereinafter.

These above-mentioned problems in connecting and operating the remote input-output devices with the CSCF's known heretofore, will be understood by one skilled in the art in view of the complexity, size and speed of these CSCF's. Also, each CSCF has had its own particular features and characteristics that have had to be taken into account in achieving the desired functional integrity. Accordingly, a brief description will be provided of the CSCF at the Brookhaven National Laboratory for an understanding of their desired shared time computer system, which is referred to hereinafter as Brooknet.

The Brooknet CSCF, comprises two CDC 6600 central computers, which as is well known in the art are described in Control Data Publication No. 60119300, November 1964. Each CDC 6600 computer has at least 10 peripheral and control processors, referred to hereinafter as PP's, which will be particularly discussed hereinafter in more detail, a central processing unit, hereinafter referred to as a CPU, a central memory having an extended core storage, hereinafter referred to as an ECS, and peripheral equipment controllers, hereinafter referred to as peripheral, e.g., such as shown in FIGS. 1 and 2.

2

The PP's are particularly important in understanding the Brooknet system, since each PP is an independent computer with 4,096 words of core storage for electrical binary signals and has a repertoire of 64 instructions. In this regard, as will be understood in more detail from the following, the PP's share access to the central memory and to 12 bi-directional input-output channels for performing the important intermediary control function of controlling the communication between the mentioned CPU and the remote input-output devices.

In this regard, it will be understood that these heretofore known PP's are conventionally combined in a multiplexing arrangement that allows them to share common hardware for arithmetic, logical, I/O, and other operations without sacrificing speed or independence. As well known in the art, this multiplexing arrangement, comprises a barrel, slot and common paths to storage (not shown for ease of explanation), and I/O channels.

The barrel is a matrix of FF's (flip-flop circuits) used to hold the quantities in the operating registers of the PP's and to give each a turn to use the execution hardware in the slow adders, shift network, etc. The quantities in the barrel shift from slot output to slot input. Each time a processor's (i.e., a PP's) data enters the slot, a portion of the instruction is executed, as shown in drawings 60119300 of the above-mentioned CDC publication.

A trip around the barrel requires 1,000 nsec (one major cycle), of which each processor's (i.e., PP's) data spend 900 nsec. in the barrel and 100 nsec. in the slot. Each PP has its own independent 4,096 word memory that may be referenced once each major cycle (once each trip around the barrel).

The PP's read data from the above-mentioned remote input-output devices, perform preliminary arithmetic and logical operations, send data and programs to the central memory in the form of binary electrical signals, assign tasks to the CPU, read the CPU results from the central memory, and send results to external storage, comprising conventional magnetic tapes, disc files, etc., or to the mentioned conventional remote input-output devices, or conventional line printers, display consoles, etc.

Characteristics of the PP's are:
— 4,096 word magnetic core storage (12-bits)
Random access, coincident current
Major cycle - 1,000 ns
Minor Cycle - 100 ns
— At least 12 bi-directional input-output channels
All channels available to all PP's
Maximum transfer rate per channel - one word/major cycle
— Real-time clock (period 4,096 major cycles)
— Instructions
  Arithmetic
  Logical
  Input-Output (i.e. I/O)
  Central memory read/write
  Exchange jump
— Average instruction execution time — two major cycles
— Indirect addressing
— Indexed addressing

30

3,692,989

3

Timing for the operations of the mentioned PP's which is conventional, comprises a four-phase master clock located on a PP chassis (1). Four 25 nsec. pulses issue each minor cycle to control movement of data and instructions. A storage sequence control system, timed by the four-phase clock, controls storage references and defines the PP's.

The master clock, comprises a TD module and a TI module. To form the 25 μsec clock pulses, a pulse from the TD is ANDed with a similar pulse that has been delayed and inverted by the TI. This results in a series of electrical pulses (primary clock) that fan out through TC modules for use as timing control. In addition to forming the clock pulses on the above-mentioned PP chassis, the master clock sends electrical pulses to another PP chassis (5) and from there to all the other PP chasis. On each chassis, the incoming electrical clock pulses form a clock system similar to the first above-mentioned PP chasis (1). Synchronization of all the clocks on all the chassis provides the same times 00 on all chassis.

The above-mentioned barrel (not shown for ease of explanation) contains A, P, Q and K registers for each of the PP's. The functions of these four registers in the barrel, comprise:

A (18 bits) — A holds one operand for add, shift, logical and selective operations. The 18-bit quantity in A may be an arithmetic operand, central memory address, or an I/O function or data word.

P (12 bits) — P is the program address register. (P) is also used as a data address in certain I/O and central instructions.

Q (12 bits) — Q holds the d portion of instructions or may hold a data word when d is an address.

K (nine bits) — K holds the F portion of an instruction word and the trip count (the number of times an instruction has been around the barrel).

The A register in the barrel receives the result of add, shift, logical or selective operations in the slot. This quantity may be stored, returned to the slot unaltered or used to condition other operations. A is conventionally tested to determine its sign and whether it is zero, non-zero or one. The result of these tests maybe used to condition jump or for other instructions. The quantity in A may be a full 18-bit central address or a 12-bit peripheral word (in which case the upper six bits will be zero).

The connections to A in the barrel are:

Outputs —

A → M - (A) may be sent as a data function word on one of the I/O channels.

A → Central Address Register - (A) is the central memory address in central read and write and exchange jump instructions.

A → Y - For a store instruction, (A) is sent to Y and then to storage.

A → Translation networks.

Inputs

X → A — The content of the central program address register is sent to the peripheral X register every minor cycle. A 27 instruction sends X to A and enables a PP to monitor the progress of the central program.

R → A — An input to A instruction gates a word from an I/O channel into A.

4

Fd → A — A data word from storage is entered into A by the Fd → A path.

A → A — When the quantity in A is to be returned to the slot unaltered, the A → A gate is enabled.

The P register holds the program address and is not changed in the barrel (except by Dead Start) which will accordingly be briefly described hereinafter). (P) is sent to a storage unit from a stage 6 in the barrel. This allows time to read a word from storage and make it available at slot time. (P) is sent to the G register, which feeds all storage and address or S registers. When a jump is called for, P is sent to Q from a barrel stage 12. Q is then altered by the Q-adder in the slot and the new address returns to P at the first stage of the barrel.

The Q-register holds the d portion of an instruction and has several outputs to translation networks that make channel selections for I/O instructions. When d is an address (Q) is sent from the slot to P in the barrel and the word obtained from that address is entered into Q in the slot. When a jump is called for, the quantity in Q is added to or subtracted from (P) in the Q-adder and the result sent to P. When an instruction calls for an 18-bit operand, the lower six bits of Q are sent to the upper six bits of A to form the 18-bit quantity dm.

The K-register holds the portion of an instruction word and a 3-bit trip count that sequences the execution of an instruction. K is translated at two different times during a trip around the barrel; first to determine if a storage reference is needed, and second, to provide the proper commands at the slot. During the barrel trip in which a new instruction is being read from storage, a translation of K = 00X enables translations from Fd in the storage cycle path to be used in place of K translations. This eliminates the need for a separate "Read Next Instruction" trip through the barrel and allows certain instructions to be read from storage and executed all in one trip. The K = 00X translation arises from the fact that K clears at the end of each instruction.

Concerning the mentioned slot, a brief description thereof will additionally help understand the operation of the above-described PP's with particular reference to the mentioned particular features and characteristics of the CDC 6600 computers. In this regard, this slot, which is illustrated in drawings 60119300 of the above-mentioned CDC publication, contains the execution hardware for the mentioned registers A, P, Q and K for the PP's. Each processor is allowed one minor cycle in the slot during every major cycle. Included in the slot are:

A Adder Shift Network Logical Circuits Selective Circuits

P Incrementor Inputs from P or Q in the barrel

Q Adder Input Path from Fd

K 3-bit Trip Counter Input from F K = 340 Gate

As A, P, Q and K enter the slot, K translations (started earlier in the barrel) become available and a portion (or all) of an instruction is executed. The results are gated back into the barrel to be stored, used again, or sent to I/O equipment.

A brief description of the heretoforeknown storage sequence control, which relates to the operation of the PP's, is also pertinent to an understanding of the particular features and characteristics of the CDC 6600's

31

5

which add to the immensity and complexity of the heretofore known problems in connecting the remote input-output devices to the Brooknet CSCF.

In this regard, timing of the memory references is controlled by the Storage Sequence Control, which is a timing chain of FF's gated by clock pulses. As a "1" passes down the chain, each FF is set for one minor cycle during which it issues commands to the storage logic. This chain reinitiates itself after each cycle and runs continuously. One memory reference is initiated each minor cycle.

The stages of the storage sequence control, a typical stage "a" being described below, are numbered according to the PP (processor) for which they initiate a memory reference, the references of a typical stage "a" being overlapped by the Storage Sequence Control. The commands issued by the first half of a typical stage are:

G   S, Storage *a*
Clear Z, Storage *a* + 1
Set Z, Storage *a* + 5
Enable Sense, Storage *a* + 7

The second half of state "a" issues commands:

Read, *a*
Write, *a* + 5
Stop Read, *a* + 6
Stop Write, *a* + 1

These commands and other signals from the storage sequence control define and separate the PP's.

It will also be understood by one skilled in the art hereof, that the reset circuit that reinitiates the storage sequence control, senses whether stages 0 – 8 are set, and if not, stage 0 is reinstated just after stage nine has issued its commands.

In like regard, a memory reference is initiated from stage 6 in the barrel, so that information from memory is available at slot time. Thus, a memory reference for processor 0 (storage 0) is initiated while processor 5 is in the slot.

A short additional description of the above-mentioned PP memory will also aid in understanding the above-mentioned problems and complexity in connecting the Brooknet CSCF with any desired remote input-output device. In this regard, the PP's have in addition to their own core-storage units, as mentioned above, their own address register (S), sense amplifiers, and restoration register (Z). However, these storage units share a common memory cycle path and common paths to and from the barrel. Each PP makes one memory reference each major cycle. When no memory reference is called for by the current instruction, address 0000 is read and restored.

The above-mentioned PP common memory cycle path warrants a further comment, as will be understood in more detail hereinafter. These common memory cycle paths receive data from the memories via the sense merge, as will be understood by one skilled in the art. To this end, the inputs to the sense merge from the sense amplifiers, are a logical "1" (0.2v) when sense is not enabled. When a PP's (processor's s sense amplifier is enabled, the outputs of the PS modules are allowed to go from +1.2v for a sensed "0." 1." Tf the core switches, the sense amplifier output goes to "0.2v "1". The AND combination of logical "1's" from unselected PP's (processors), even or odd sense, enable, and "1"

6

bits from the selected PP's (processors), sense amplifiers, sets the word from memory into the F*d* register in the memory cycle path.

Also, with regard to the memory cycle path, this path sends information to the barrel, I/O channels, translators and central write pyramid which will be briefly discussed hereinafter, and receives information from the barrel, central read pyramid, and I/O channels. Outputs from F*d* in the memory cycle path are translated and used to form commands when $K = 00X$ (read next instruction trip).

In this regard also, the memory cycle path (either the read word or a new word) is fanned out from the Y-register to the Z-registers. The set signal from the storage sequence control, gates the complement of the word to be stored into the proper Z-register.

Since the K-register, A-adder and shift network are important in understanding the above, a few short comments thereon will be added. In this regard, an example of K in the above-mentioned slot, comprises a three-bit counter for the lower three bits and a fan-in for the upper six bits. The advance K-signal to the trip counter is enabled by instruction translations. In some instructions, the advance K signal is controlled by signals that indicate status, e.g., the 5×0 trip may be skipped by all 5x instructions if $d = 0$, and when $K = 732$, K may be advanced only if the I/O channel is empty and active and $A = 1$.

Likewise with regard to the K register, the three-bit trip controls the sequence of operations for each instruction and is sometimes changed by gates other than the trip counter. For example, for a central write instruction (63), K is changed from 637 to 633 to repeat the sequence of commands and to send another word. When a 63 instruction is completed, K is changed from 637 to 733 to finalize the instruction and obtain the next instruction from storage.

Finally, with regard to the K-register, the fan-in to the upper six bits of K allows the instruction code F to be entered into K from storage. The K → K path allows another trip around the barrel for the present instruction. The path $K = 340$ is used to replace instructions that automatically use the store instruction **34** to accomplish the store portion of the replace instructions.

Now the A-ADDER will be briefly discussed in the above-mentioned context for understanding the operation of the PP's and the consequent problems of connecting and operating the Brooknet CSCF with any desired remote input-output device. In this regard, as will be understood by one skilled in the art, the A-ADDER is used to execute add, subtract, selective clear, logical product, and logical difference instructions, as illustrated in drawings 60119300 of the above-mentioned CDC publication. Parts of the A-adder are also used to enter a word into the shift network and gate the result back to the barrel. The quantity in A in the barrel is complemented when it enters the slot. When no operation on A is called for, (A) is complemented, enters the A-adder, is added to zero, and the result is recomplemented at the output. The Add gate in the QD modules is enabled except when Selective Clear, Logical Product, or Shift commands are enabled.

The following table will make this clear to one skilled in the art with regard to this A ADDER:

3,692,989

7

TABLE I

Add

For an add instruction (A) is complemented and entered into the A-input register. The second operand is also complemented and entered into the B-input register. The two quantities in the input registers, taken as positive are added and the sum is recomplemented as it is gated out of the QD modules to the barrel.

Subtract

For subtract instructions, the minuend, (A) is complemented as it enters the adder. The subtrahend is entered into B without being complemented and the two quantities are added as in an add instruction.

Selective Clear

For selective clear, the complement of A and the true value of d are entered into the adder and both the selective and the logical product gates are enabled.

Logical Product

For logical product instructions, both A and d (or dm) are complemented before entering the adder and both the logical product and the selective gates are enabled.

Logical Difference

For logical difference instructions, the complement of A and the true value of the second operand enter the adder and only the selective gate is enabled.

Referring in like regard to the Shift Network for an understanding of the operation of the PP's by one skilled in the art, the shift network (10) provides for shifting the number in A up to 31 places left or right. Left shift is circular with the high order bits re-entering A at the low order end. Right shift is end-off with low order bits discarded as they shift out of the A-register and with no sign extension. Thus, a left shift of 18 is equivalent to no shift, and a right shift of 18 clears the A-register.

It will be understood that the Shift Network is static. In this regard, the content of A enters the register at time IV, each bit follows a path established by static translations of the six-bit shift count in d, and the result enters A in the barrel at the next time IV. The input to the Shift Network from the A-input register in the A-adder (the content of that register, which is the complement of A), is recomplemented before entering the shift register. The output of the Shift Network is gated back to the barrel by way of the output modules (QD) of the A-adder. It will be noted also, that the quantity in A is shifted but the result is gated to the barrel only when the current instruction is a shift.

Likewise, with regard to the shift Network, if d is positive (00–37$_8$) the shift is left and the shift count is the content of d. If d is negative (40–77$_8$) the shift is right and the shift count is the complement of the number in d.

Likewise, with regard to the Shift Network, at the first stage of the Shift Network, d_4 and d_5 are tested to determine whether the shift is greater or less than 16 and whether it is left or right. If the shift is 16 or greater, a shift of 16 is made at this point and the result then enters the rest of the Shift Network. It is also noted that bits $d_0 - d_3$ are tested with d_3 to set up paths through the rest of the network.

8

Finally, in understanding the complexity of the heretofore known problems in connecting the remote input-output devices to the Brooknet CSCF, reference is made to the fact that the PP's communicate in several ways with central memory and the CPU. In this regard, the PP's may read the CPU's program address, tell the CPU to jump to a given central memory address for its next instruction, or read from or write into central memory, as is well known in the art.

To this end, the Central Program Monitor bears mentioning, since the 18-bit CPU program address is sent to the Central Program Monitor register on chassis 1 every minor cycle. In this regard also, a Read Program Address instruction (27) sends the central address to the A register. Thus, the progress of a central program may be monitored by any PP acting as a peripheral and control processor.

Also, with regard to this Central Program Monitor, Exchange Jump, Central Read, and Central Write instructions all use the content of A as a central memory address. (A) is unconditionally sent to address control in the CPU every minor cycle. This quantity is recognized and used as a central memory address only if accompanied by a Central Read, Central Write, or Exchange Jump signal. It is additionally noted that the Central Busy FF indicates when a reference to central is in progress. Also, a central busy condition prevents initiating a central reference until one in progress is completed.

Now, with regard to the Exchange Jump, an exchange jump instruction is used to command the CPU to stop the program it is executing and go to a central memory location specified by the instruction. An exchange jump may be issued by any PP so long as the Central Busy FF is clear. The instruction sends an Exchange Jump signal to the CPU and sets the Central Busy FF. The Exchange Jump signal tells the CPU to recognize the 18-bit address sent from the PP and to perform an exchange jump. After the CPU has performed the exchange jump and started a new program, it sends a Resume signal that clears the Central Busy FF to allow another central reference. If a PP tries to issue an Exchange Jump instruction while the Central Busy FF is set, the PP must wait until the previous central reference is completed and the Central Busy FF is cleared.

Now, regarding the above, with particular reference to Central Read, the Central Read instruction allows a PP to obtain one word (60 bits) or a block of words from Central Memory. The instruction sends a Central Read signal to central address control enabling it to use the 18-bit quantity from A as a central memory address. At the same time, the Central Busy FF is set to inhibit other references to central until the read word is received.

As will be understood in more detail hereinafter, when a 60-bit word has heretofore been conventionally sent by central to the Central Read Pyramid (shown in FIG. 2), it has been accompanied by two control signals, an accept that clears the Central Busy FF, and a signal that sets the C^5 Full FF. Each rank of the mentioned Central Read Pyramid C^1 – C$_5$ has had an associated Full/Empty FF used to control the flow of data through the pyramid. C^5 full and C^4 Empty has enabled the PP doing the read instruction to send the upper 12

33

3,692,989

9

bits of C⁸ to memory and the lower 48 bits to C⁴, as will be understood in the art. Subsequent steps in the central Read instruction has resulted in stepping the central word down through the pyramid and storing the rest of the central word as 12-bit peripheral words. Each step in this storage procedure has required that the next lower rank in the heretofore known pyramid be empty before a transfer was made. No Central Read instruction conventionally has been issued until C⁸ Full FF and Central Busy FF have been clear. However, as many as five central memory words, in different stages or disassembly, have been in the Central Read Pyramid at one time. A read instruction for which the proper full and empty conditions have not been met has required waiting until previous instructions have progressed further and conditions have been met. In regard also to Central Read, as will be understood by one skilled in the art, it is noted that a 60 instruction heretofore read only one central memory word and stored it as five peripheral words. Likewise, a 61 instruction read a block of words specified by (d). In either instruction the first central memory address has been specified by (A). For a 60 instruction, d has specified the peripheral address at which the upper 12 bits of the peripheral word have been stored; the next lower 12 bits going to d + 1, etc. For a 61 instruction, (d) has given the number of central words to be read and m has been the address for the upper 12 bits of the first central word.

Central write instructions, which also will be understood as being related to the above, send one 60-bit word or a block of 60-bit words to Central Memory. In this regard, each 60-bit word that has been conventionally sent to Central Memory has been assembled in the central Write Pyramid known heretofore from five 12-bit peripheral words. A Central Write instruction has assembled a 60-bit word and sent the word and a Central Write signal to central address control and of disassembly, the Central Busy FF. The Central Write signal has enabled central address control to accept the 60-bit word and to store it at the address specified by (A). When the word has been stored, an accept signal has been sent back to clear the Central Busy FF. Up to four Central Write instructions could heretofore have been in progress at one time with portions of four different words in D¹- D⁴. D⁵ has been an output network only and could not store a word. The first 12-bit word has gone to D¹ and has been the upper 12 bits of the 60-bit word. When a second 12-bit word has gone to D², D¹ has also sent to D². When the fifth word has gone to D⁵, the 48 bits in D⁴ have also been sent to D⁵ and the 60-bit word has been sent to central.

The operation of the Input/Output is as follows. Each of the independent data channels 0–14 (see FIG. 2), can handle 12-bit words at a maximum rate of one word every major cycle, which is equivalent to a 1 megacycle rate. Each channel has an Active/Inactive FF and a Full/Empty FF which indicate channel status to the PP's. Any channel may be used by any PP, but the external equipment to a channel, as is conventional, is wired in and may be assigned to another channel only by changing cable connections.

The conventional lines of a data channel are listed in the following table II:

10

TABLE II

INPUT	OUTPUT
Data or Status Reply (12 bits)	Data or Function Word (12 bits)
Active	Active
Inactive (Disconnect)	Inactive
Full	Full
Empty	Empty
	MC

In addition, as illustrated in Drawings 60119300 of the above-referenced CDC publication, two clock signals are available to the external equipment: a 1 mc/sec clock and a 10 mc clock. The clock pulses are 25 nsec wide, as are all data and control signals (except master clear). Controllers for each piece of external equipment (or group thereof) perform the conversion between the 6600 pulse signals and the signals required by the I/O devices.

A data channel may be used for communication between PP's if the channel is selected for input by one PP and for output by another PP. The status of the data channels may be sensed by instructions 64–67: jump to m if channel d active, etc.

Master Clear (i.e., MC) can next be more particularly described. In this regard, an MC signal is generated only by a Dead Start Circuit so as to remove all equipment selections except Dead Start and to set all channels to the Active and Empty Condition (i.e., read for input). MC is a 1 μsec pulse that is repeated every 255μsec. while the Dead Start switch is on.

The importance of Disconnect (75), can be described as follows. A disconnect instruction clears the channel Active FF if the latter is set and sends an inactive pulse to the equipment on that channel. Given a disconnect instruction for an already inactive channel, the processor that issued the disconnect will cause the important problem of a "hang up," which means that the PP will not be able to continue until the channel is re-acticated. The importance of this "hang up" will be discussed in more detail hereinafter, and also will be understood hereinafter in connection with the below described invention.

Function (76 or 77) can be described as follows. A function instruction sends a 12-bit function code (from A or Fd) on the data lines and sends a Function signal. This function instruction also sets the Active and Full FF's for the channel but does not send Active and Full pulses. Upon receipt of the function code, the external equipment sends an Inactive (disconnect signal, clearing the Active FF in the data channel, which in turn clears the Full FF. If a function instruction is given for an active channel, the PP will "hang-up" until the channel is de-activated. As will be understood by one skilled in the art, it is advantageous to avoid such "-hang-ups" in a fail-safe manner in connecting and operating the remote input-output devices of Brooknet with the CSCF. In this regard, important advantages of avoiding such "hang-ups" will be understood in more detail hereinafter.

With regard to Activate (74), an Activate instruction sends an Active signal on the channel and sets the Active FF if the channel is inactive. If an Activate instruction is given for a channel that is already active, the PP that issued the instruction will "hang-up" until the channel is inactivated, e.g., by another PP or by an Inactive (disconnect) signal from external equipment on the channel. The importance of this "hang-up," like the

3,692,989

11

other above-mentioned "hang-ups" will be understood by one skilled in the art, since these "hang-ups" have presented highly complex if not insurmountable problems in connecting some of the above-mentioned remote input-output devices to the Brooknet CSCF.

Regarding the above in relation to one example of the Data Input Sequence, an external device sends data to the processor (PP) by way of the controller according to the steps illustrated by the following Table III:

TABLE III

1. The processor places a function word in the channel register and sets the full flag and the channel active flag. Coincidentally, the processor sends the word and a function signal to all controllers. The function signal tells the controllers to sample the word as a function code rather than a data word. The code selects a controller and a mode of operation. Non-selected controllers clear, leaving only the selected one turned on.

2. The controller sends an inactive signal to the processor indicating acceptance of the function code. The signal drops the channel active flag, which in turn drops the full flag and clears the channel register.

3. The processor sets the channel active flag and sends an active signal to the controller, which signals the device to start sending data.

4. The device reads a word and then sends the word to the channel register with a full signal, which sets the channel full flag.

5. The processor stores the word, drops the full flag, and returns an empty signal indicating acceptance of the word. The device clears its data register and prepares to send the next word.

6. Steps 4 and 5 repeat for each word transferred.

7. At the end of the transfer, the controller clears its active condition and sends an inactive signal to the processor to indicate the end of the data. The signal clears the channel active flag to disconnect the controller and the processor from the channel.

8. As an alternative, the processor may choose to disconnect from the channel before the device has sent all of its data. The processor does this by dropping the active flag and sending an inactive flag to the controller, which immediately clears its active condition and sends no more data, although the device may continue to the end of its data record or cycle (e.g., a magnetic tape unit would continue to the end of the record and stop in the record gap).

One example of the Status Request, which is also relevant to the above-mentioned problems, comprises a special one word data input transfer in which an external remote input-output device indicates a ready or error condition to a processor (PP, according to the steps illustrated by the following Table IV:

TABLE IV

1. The processor places a function word in the channel register and sets the full flag and the channel active flag. Coincidentally, the processor sends the word and function signal to all controllers. The function signal tells all the controllers to sample the word and defines the word as a function code rather than a data word. The code selects a controller and places the controller in status mode. Non-selected controllers clear, leaving only the selected one turned on.

12

2. The controller sends an inactive signal to the processor indicating acceptance of the status function code. The signal drops the channel active flag, which in turn drops the full flag and clears the channel register.

3. The processor sets the channel active flag and sends an active signal to the controller, which signals the device to send the status word.

4. The controller sends the status word to the channel register with a full signal that sets the channel full flag.

5. The processor stores the word, drops the full flag, and returns to an empty signal indicating acceptance of the word.

6. The processor drops the channel active flag to disconnect the channel and sends an inactive signal to the controller to disconnect the controller.

In examples of the Data Output Sequence, the processor sends data to an external device according to steps illustrated by the following:

1. The processor places a function word in the channel register and sets the full flag and the channel active flag. Coincidentally, the processor sends the word and a function signal to all devices. The function signal tells all the controllers to sample the word and identifies the word as a function code rather than a data word. The code selects a controller and a mode of operation. Non-selected controllers clear, leaving only the selected one turned on.

2. The controller sends an inactive signal to the processor, indicating acceptance of the function code. The signal drops the channel active flag, which in turn drops the full flag and clears the channel register.

3. the processor sets the channel active flag and sends an active signal to the controller, which signals the device that data flow is starting.

4. The processor places a data word in the channel register and sets the full flag. Coincidentally, the processor sends the word and a full signal to the controller.

5. The controller accepts the word and sends an empty signal to the processor, where the signal clears the channel register and drops the full flag.

6. After the last word is transferred and acknowledged by the controller with an empty signal, the processor drops the channel active signal to the controller to turn it off.

A brief description of Dead Start, Load, Sweep and Dump relate to an understanding of the heretofore known operation of the above-mentioned elements, with particular reference to the initial operation of the PP's.

Dead Start is a system used initially to start the Brooknet CSCF computers to dump the contents of the PP memories to a conventional printer or other conventional output device, or to sweep the mentioned memories without executing instructions. The Dead Start panel, comprises a 12 × 12 matrix of toggle switches, a Sweep-Load-Dump switch, a Dead Start switch, and memory margin switches that are used for maintenance checks.

Initially, to load the programs and the data, the Sweep-Load-Dump switch is put into the Load position. The matrix of toggle switches is set to a 12-word program (up = "1," down = "0") In one example, when the Dead-Start switch is turned on, a 1 μsec Dead Start pulse performs the following Table V, which will also be understood from drawings 60119300 of the above-mentioned CDC publication:

TABLE V

1. Assigns to each PP the corresponding I/O channel.
2. Sets all channels to Active and Empty.
3. Sets K for all processors (PP's) to 712 (Input).
4. Sends an MC on all channels.
5. Sets A and P for all processors to zero (A being then set to 10000_8 at stage 10 in the barrel).

The Dead Start pulse is repeated every $225\mu sec$ while the DS switch is on. To start the machine, the DS switch is normally turned on momentarily, and then is turned off. Recycling of the DS pulse is controlled by the Real Time Clock; the pulse is formed by ANDing the DS switch in the ON position with 10 bits of the Real Time Clock.

When the Dead Start controller on channel 0 receives the MC sent by Dead Start, this controller sends a Full pulse but no data. When processor 0 receives the Full, the processor stores the content of the channel 0 input register (all zeros) in location 0000 and sends an Empty pulse to the Dead Start controller. The Dead Start controller then acts as an input device, sending 12, 12-bit words from the switch matrix, these words being stored in locations 0001 – 00014$_8$. After the last word, the Dead Start controller sends a disconnect that causes processor 0 (i.e., PP–O) to exit from the 712 instruction. PP–O reads location 0000, adds one to its contents and goes to 0001 for the next instruction. This PP–O then executes the 12-word (or less) program, which normally is a control program to load information and begin operation. The other PP's are still set to 712 (waiting to input when their channels become full) and may receive data from PP–O via their assigned I/O channels.

Regarding the above-mentioned Sweep, if the DS switch is operated with the Sweep-Load-Dump switch in the Sweep position, all PP's are set to a 505 instruction and P registers set to 0000. Since the 50 instruction does not require five trips around the barrel, there is no logic to clear or advance K from 505. The 50x translation of K causes all PP's to sweep through their memories, reading and restoring without executing instructions. This is a maintenance routine and may be used to check the operation of the memory logic.

In one example of the above-mentioned Dump, the Dead Start with the Sweep-Load-Dump switch in the Dump position causes the following steps illustrated by the following Table VI:

TABLE VI

1. Sets all PP's to 732
2. Sends MC on all channels.
3. Holds channel O Active and Empty.
4. Assigns each PP to its corresponding I/O Channel.
5. Sets all A an P registers to O.

In regard to the above mentioned steps of Dump, all PP's sense the Empty and Active condition on their assigned channels, output the content of their address 0000, set their I/O channels to Full, and wait for an Empty. All PP's advance P by one and reduce A by one (A = 7776$_8$). Channel 0, which is assigned to PP – O, is held Empty by the Dump Switch. PP–O, thereupon cycles through the 732

instruction until A = 1 and then goes to memory location 0001 for its next instruction. PP–O has sent its entire memory content on channel 0 although no I/O device was selected to receive this memory content. PP–O is now free to execute a dump program, which must have been previously stored in memory 0, beginning at location 0001.

Other elements of the Brooknet CSCF CDC 6600 computers, which are also discussed in detail in the above-mentioned CDC publication, comprise the Console Display Controller, Disk System Controller, Card Reader Controller, Magnetic Tape Transport Controller, Printer Controller, and Card Punch Controller. In this regard, the operation of each of the described CDC 6600's is performed by well known hardware and non-mental software, as will be understood from the above described description by one skilled in the art. In this regard, it will be understood that one conventional software system for these CDC 6600's is the SCOPE 3.1 system described in detail in the SCOPE 3 Manual, which is published by the Control Data Corporation as Reference Manual Publication No. 60189400, dated Apr. 1, 1968. To this end, it will be understood that these conventional programs and other non-mental programs can be stored in the PP memories and the Central Memory of the CPU. Also to this end, all PP's may use this Central Memory for Supplementary storage or inter-communication control. Thus, for example, the Central Memory addresses are generated by the CPU and all PP's, as illustrated in the 60119300 drawings of the above-mentioned CDC publication.

As described in that publication, the Central Memory involves the conventional operations and elements, comprising: Address-Data Flow; Go Control; Address Flow; Storage Sequence Control; Data Flow, write Control; Data Distributor; Read Distributor, Write Distributor.

From the above, it will be understood that immense and complex problems have heretofore been involved in connecting the mentioned remote input-output devices to the described Brooknet CSCF even though conventional devices and steps have been involved. In this regard the functional integrity of each an every one of the remote input-output devices, the proper scheduling of their operations on a regular priority basis, and/or the physical operation with the described CPU via the described data channels and PP's, has heretofore involved the full testing of the functional integrity of these remote input-output devices by the execution of the PP instructions that effect each remote input-output device. Thus, for example, the behavior of these instructions could be compared with their expected behavior to determined if the remote device was functioning properly. However, this has involved writing logical programs made up of PP instructions in order to test the functional integrity of each of the remote devices, and ordinarily the writing of these programs has been very time consuming, difficult, and expensive. Moreover, there has been no assurance that these logical programs and/or the instructions were protected. In this regard, protected means:

    1. The PP instructions in the program in a particular PP, i.e., the particular non-mental PP software program, will not suspend the operation of that PP even if the remote device being tested malfunc-

3,692,989

15	16

tions, i.e., the hardware (or the non-mental software of the remote device if it is a computer) malfunctions;

2. The instructions in the above-referred to PP program will not destroy any other part of that program or any part of the PP resident programs in any other PP due to logical program errors.

It will be understood, therefore, that the heretofore known diagnostics have been expensive, difficult, and time-consuming, have lacked fail-safety, and have also frequently required the dedication of the CSCF to the diagnostic tasks, which has resulted in the still further expense of shutting down the entire CSCF and the loss of the valuable production time thereof.

It is an object of this invention, therefore, to provide a diagnostic that does not devote the entire CSCF to the diagnostic;

It is another object to provide a non-mental diagnostic process that is carried out exclusively by the CSCF;

It is another object to provide continuously self-diagnosing computer hardware for preventing failures, and for diagnosing, recording and/or correcting failures in the CSCF and in the remote input-output devices for continuously maintaining communications back and forth between such devices and the CSCF;

It is a further object to improve the Brooknet computer system by providing a diagnostic that functions as a standard job while the Brooknet system is operating to perform many other standard jobs;

It is a still further object to provide a fail-safe, non-mental, diagnostic, software package, referred to hereinafter as Quest, having its own language for maintaining the operation of the CSCF in the Brooknet computer system so that new or experimental input-output or other such remote devices can be added to the Brooknet system in a relatively trouble-free and expeditious manner without dedicating the entire CSCF to the diagnoses of the failures thereof.

In this regard, some of the objectives of QUEST are to provide:

a. A hardware orientated diagnostic language of high enough level to allow the user ease in writing, debugging and testing his (diagnostic) -user's program;

b. A generated code that is free from logical program errors;

c. A generated code that will not cause the executing PP to suspend its operation due to peripheral hardware malfunctions;

d. Means for responding to operator intervention;

e. A software package written substantially in an assembly language for a particular computer, e.g., the CDC 6600, which is described in "Control Data Corporation Customer Engineering" Control Data Publication Number 60119300, November, 1964;

f. A software package, comprising several subprograms, the principal ones of which are:

Phase I - Compilation

    i. TEST — which is written in a sufficiently high language for calling the proper subprograms into the process, and listing the user's program on the output file;

    ii. COMPI — for actually translating and communicating the user's program from the special QUEST language into the PP instruction in a particular PP, noting any logical program errors, and taking the proper action;

    iii. ERROR — which,upon encountering an error, is called for by COMPI to list the error in the appropriate place in the user's output file;

Phase II - Actual Running of Diagnostic

    iv. PPMTR — which monitors the execution or running of the diagnostic (user's program), receives the product of Phase I, and later passes the diagnostic on to another subprogram, referred to hereinafter as AYN, and (the product of Phase I being a block of code that represents the user's program translated into PP instructions) directs all recovery procedures in the event of hardware malfunctions;

    v. AYN — which, unlike the previously mentioned subprogram (iv), resides in the PP along with the translated user's program (diagnostic), communicates the status of the (diagnostic) user's program to PPMTR, and records all errors and responds to operator intervention during execution of the (diagnostic) user's program;

    vi. AIK — which, if communication between AYN and PPMTR is severed, represents a PP program that is called by PPMTR, which determines why the execution of the (diagnostic) user's program is suspended, and which attempts to correct the malfunction as directed by PPMTR.

In regard to the latter, it is an object of the interaction of the Phase II subprograms to insure that the operating system of the CSCF is undisturbed, regardless of the behavior of the hardware of the CSCF or the remote devices connected thereto, during the execution of the (diagnostic) user's program, thus preventing dedication of the CSCF solely to the (diagnostic) user's program, and providing for no loss of valuable CSCF production time.

Furthermore, it is an object of QUEST to:

1. detect malfunctions and to allow the execution of instructions to continue;

2. run as a subsystem of the CDC SCOPE 3 operating system, and be dependent upon the various system functions that SCOPE provides; and

3. specifically to test hardware attached to the CDC 6600 computer and which conforms to the particular I/O structure of that computer.

SUMMARY OF THE INVENTION

This invention which was made in the course of, or under a contract with the U.S. Atomic Energy Commission, provides a computer diagnostic that does not require dedication of the entire computer. More particularly, the computer diagnostic of this invention keeps in operation a time-sharing CSCF and many remote devices connected thereto, such as a plurality of computers, while diagnosing and/or preventing failures in the hardware and/or non-mental software internally and externally of the CSCF, and without dedicating the entire CSCF to the diagnostic. In one embodiment, the diagnostic hardware of this invention comprises a portion of the CPU, and two PP's that communicate with each other, the CPU, and the remote devices connected to the CSCF in a self-diagnosing system for maintaining the operation of the Brooknet system without dedicating the entire CSCF to

17

18

the diagnostic. In another aspect, this invention provides a fail-safe diagnostic for the Brooknet system. With the proper selection of components and steps, as described in more detail hereinafter, the desired diagnostic is achieved. To this end, this invention contemplates in a computer system, comprising a plurality of data channels selectively coupled to a plurality of peripheral processors that are selectively coupled to a central processor, the method of analyzing the functional integrity of a device coupled to one of said data channels, comprising the steps of:

a. providing to the central processor a first stored program that monitors the state of a first one of said peripheral processors coupled to the said one of said data channels, and activates a second stored program in the said first one of said peripheral processors, said second stored program providing checks on the validity of the commands to and the validity of the responses from the said device, and

b. when the said first one of said peripheral processors becomes inoperative in response to an invalid response from the said device, then couples a second of said peripheral processors to the said channel and activates a third stored program in said second one of said peripheral processors, for restoring the functional ability of the said first one of said peripheral processors, and provides sequential time-based output information relating to the state of the said device, whereby, the said computer system retains its normal functional integrity independent of the functional integrity of the said device.

In another aspect, this invention involves the operation of the diagnostics on a regular job priority basis with other jobs in the CSCF.

The above and further novel features and objects of this invention will become apparent from the following detailed description of one embodiment of this invention when the same is read in connection with the accompanying drawings, and the novel features will be particularly pointed out in the appended claims.

BRIEF DESCRIPTION OF THE DRAWINGS

In the drawings, where like elements are referenced alike:

FIG. 1 is a partial schematic illustration of one embodiment of the apparatus of this invention;

FIG. 2 is a partial schematic illustration of one arrangement of the computers of FIG. 1;

FIG. 3 is a partial schematic illustration of one arrangement of the data channels of FIG. 2;

FIG. 4 is a partial schematic illustration of one arrangement of one data channel of FIG. 3;

FIG. 5 is a partial schematic illustration of one condition of the data channel of FIG. 4;

FIG. 6, which is comprised of FIGS. 6a and 6b, is a partial schematic illustration of another condition of the data channel of FIG. 4;

FIG. 7 is a partial schematic illustration of still another condition of the data channel of FIG. 4;

FIG. 8 is a partial schematic illustration of the apparatus of FIG. 2, showing in simplified form the apparatus of this invention.

DETAILED DESCRIPTION OF ONE EMBODIMENT

This invention provides a fail-safe diagnostic for the Brooknet shared-time computer system described above for the operation thereof without dedicating the entire CSCF to the diagnostic. As such, this invention provides a diagnostic for a shared time computer system for binary signals, comprising a large CSCF having two CDC 6600 computers, which form a CPU and ECS as described in detail in Control Data Publication Number 60119300, November 1964, and which connects PPs across data channels to a large number of remote Brooknet computers and other remote binary input-output devices. Thus, the principles of this invention are applicable to many computer systems, computer types and shared-time computer applications where a fail-safe diagnostic is desired without dedicating the entire computer to the diagnostic. Also, while one application and one embodiment of this invention are described herein in connection with Brooknet, as will be understood in more detail hereinafter, this invention is useful in many Brooknet or other applications where diagnostic hardware and non-mental software are required for a time-sharing computer system.

Referring now to FIG. 1, CSCF 11, comprises an extended core storage 13, referred to hereinafter as ECS 13, a first, large, digital, binary signal computer 15, comprising (in line with the above description) CDC 6600 A, a second like large computer 17, comprising a second CDC 6600 B, and peripheral equipment 19 for the CSCF for the Brooknet shared computer system 21, which has at least one remote binary signal generating input and/or output device forming an input-output station 23 for communicating incoming and outgoing binary signals between station 23 and the CSCF 11. Advantageously, this remote station 23 is part of a remote digital, binary signal computer 25 that communicates back and forth with CSCF 11. To this end, various input and/or output signals are generated in both CSCF 11 and remote computer 25 as a result of various scientific, test, experimental or other inputs or outputs, and/or the operation of various computers or other hardware and nonmental software. For ease of explanation, this invention will be described in connection with only one binary CSCF 11 and only one remote binary computer 25, but it is understood that one or many such remote computers, or other standard binary input and/or output units having a wide variety of auxilliary or peripheral equipment may be used. Thus, for example, teletype 27 and/or other means not shown, having standard binary input and output means outside CSCF 11, communicate with CSCF 11 through a computer 29, such as a PDP–8 computer, which is connected to computers 15 and 17 through switch 31 and couplers 33 and 35.

It is likewise understood, that the remote input-output computer 25 is advantageously used for a wide variety of inputs and outputs requiring real-time or other communications between two points outside CSCF 11. Thus, this invention is useful in connection with a wide variety of remote means outside CSCF 11 e.g., for scientific experimental, research, manufacturing, educational, domestic, agricultural or other applications. One system for transmitting and communicating complicated real-time experimental information

3,692,989

19

between a digital computer 25 and another means outside CSCF 11 for generating and/or receiving digital and/or analogue signals, is described in copending application Ser. No. 764,144, filed Oct. 1, 1968, now U.S. Pat. No. 3,582,901, by Cochrane and Russell, which is assigned to the assignee of this application and incorporated by reference herein. In this regard, on-line utilization of remote input-output digital computers, such as computer 25, is a relatively new phenomenon whose major impact has been in greatly improved quality of experimental data, and increased scope of nuclear experimentations. However, heretofore, large amounts of time have been necessary for programming, software and troubleshooting for each experiment. In this regard, it is enormously important to have programming systems that permit the writing of experimental programs with minimum expenditures of effort and of time, and with minimum requirements of computer expertise and troubleshooting diagnostics,e.g. of some isolated preamplifier or small malfunctioning unit, as described in YALE 3223-139, 145, 121, 130 and 129, which is also printed in Physics Today, July 1968.

The above will be understood by one skilled in the art, since the CSCF 11 and the remote input-output computer 25, involve well known communications, job priority systems, circuits and methods for generating, receiving, communicating and operating on digital information in the form of binary non-mental bits and bit streams. These bits are the smallest conceptualized units of information in binary form, and like numbers and letters are pure abstractions. However, to transmit these informational bits they must be represented in some physical form, such as electrical signals or pulses (1) or the absence of such electrical signals or pulses (0). Also, the CSCF 11 and remote computer 25 operate on or with these bits, e.g., to fetch and store the bits, and to execute various arithmetic and logical operations in connection therewith. The CSCF also operates on a regular job priority basis and it is advantageous to operate the remote computer 25 with the CSCF 11 on a regular shared time priority basis.

To this end, the CSCF 11 has a large number of elements governing the orderly flow of bits and words made of bits therethrough and back and forth with and through remote computer 25. For example, the peripheral equipment 19 advantageously comprises conventional large storage capacity but relatively slow operating discs 37 (compared to the CPU 87) and linear access tapes 39, synchronizers 41, couplers 43, controllers 45, and input and output means 47 and 49, as shown in FIG. 2. In this regard, non-mental bits corresponding to specific binary words and binary non-mental software programs are put into CSCF 11 from card readers 51 having standard card punchers 53 connected to a data channel 55 through a coupler 57. For read out purposes output 47, comprises standard printers 59 and 61 and standard print controllers 63 and 65, which are connected to a data channel 67 through coupler 69. Also, a suitable cathode ray tube oscilloscope display 71 connects with channel 73 through synchronizer 75.

It will be understood from the above that failures in communications to and from CSCF 11 and remote computer 25 may occur due to many possible human

20

errors or unforeseen problems, such as hardware or non-mental software errors or failures and/or other errors outside CSCF 11, e.g., in teletypes such as TTY 27, PDP–8 computer 25, inputs 47, or outputs 49, e.g., due to errors on disks 37 and 37'. Moreover, these failures are hard to predict due to the complicated nature of the many input and output connections and communications between CSCF 11 and remote computer 25, which e.g., connects to CSCF 11 through a channel 77 and synchronizer 79 for the desired operation in the described Brooknet system 21. An additional complication is that fact that each PP 81, which is a computer having the usual hardware for standard and non-standard software, comprising non-mental programs, is as powerful as any other PP 81, and has access to each and every other portion of the Brooknet system, comprising any portion of the remote input-output computer 25, and CSCF 11, comprising (central processing unit) CPU 87 in computers 15 and 17, which has access to ECS 13, and data channels 89, comprising the above-mentioned channels 55, 67, 73, and 77. In this regard, the bits, bit streams and binary data words coming into and out of the various above-mentioned elements due to the connection of the remote computer 25 with CSCF 11 in the Brooknet system 21, can cause the PP's 81 to "hang-up," in which case the whole CSCF 11 was heretofore down for debugging.

As an example of such a "hang-up," reference is made to FIG. 3 which illustrates remote computer 25 connected to CPU 87 through a conventional remote computer control 90, remote control adapter 91, multiplexer 93, data terminals 95 and 97, local control unit 99, synchronizer 79, which may have one or more other synchronizers 79' and channel 77, which may be connected and have access to CPU 87 through any PP 81. In this example, it is desired that these elements transfer bits and bit streams in the form of non-mental data words from remote computer 25 into CPU 87 of CSCF 11 for storing and/or fetching these data words for various non-mental arithmetical and logical operations and manual or programmed read outs in printers 59 and 61 or display 71, etc., in accordance with non-mental software instructions fed into the memories of the various components, e.g., through CR's 51 and 51', CPC's 53 and 53', teletype 27, PDP–8 29 and/or through switch 31. In this regard, this transfer of electrical signals corresponding to the bits of the bit streams and data words depends on the non-mental software to provide specific programmed non-mental instructions. Thus, for example, the hardware of remote computer 25, PP's 81 and/or CPU 87 of CSCF 11, must open and close specific switches to transfer in an orderly fashion the various bits, which correspond to the input from remote computer 25, to specific memory components of these elements, ECS 13, disc 37 or tape 39, for storage therein and fetching therefrom for the various arithmetical and logical operations desired. Consequently, the lack of the correct connections, the failure of a particular hardware component, or the lack of the correct specific non-mental instruction will prevent these elements, e.g., one of the PP's 81, from transferring the incoming bits past that element. In this example, therefore, a PP 81, e.g., PP 103, will "hang-up" due to a failure in one or

3,692,989

21

more element of some of the various pieces of hardware, or an error in one or more of the various nonmental programs.

The "hang-up" may occur in the middle of a data word, or at the beginning or end of such a word, that comprises several bits or bit streams. Therefore, incoming data would normally be lost. Also, heretofore the entire CSCF would often require complete shut-down to diagnose the failure or error, and this resulted in expensive downtime.

Should the transfer of the bits, bit streams or words to the desired location or memory be continuously selfmonitored by a portion of CPU 87 in connection with its operation with a PP, e.g., PP 103 so that every time there is a potential or actual failure of the desired transfer, a substitute non-mental data absorber automatically provides a substitute transfer to a specific substitute piece of hardware for absorption thereby, for example to and by a portion of PP 105 in accordance with this invention, the hang-up can be prevented, recorded, diagnosed, and/or removed in an orderly fashion without shutting down the entire CSCF 11 while the CSCF 11 still performs its regular or innumerable other jobs for remote computer 25, etc., and/or in connection with any of the mentioned inputsoutputs 47 and 49. To this end also, in accordance with this invention the specific piece of hardware where the hang-up occurred, e.g., PP 103, automatically self-controlled itself for revival of its service on the regular job performed thereby before the hang-up occurred therein. Additionally, the described continuous selfmonitoring of the desired transfer, e.g., of bits from remote computer 25, automatically self-regulates itself to continue independently of the original "hang-up."

In this regard it is advantageous to provide a timebased diagnostic method of operating the abovedescribed embodiment, which is illustrated in FIGS. 2 and 3 for providing self-analysis of the functional integrity of the above-mentioned remote input-output devices coupled to one of the described or other like data channels, which are collectively referred to hereinafter as channels 89. To this end, it is advantageous to connect computer 25 to CSCF 11 through channel 77 for operation of the Brooknet computer system 21. In one embodiment of an actual failure, the data channels 89 all selectively couple to all the PP's 81, and all these PP's 81 selectively couple to CPU 87 in operable association with suitable synchronizers and clocks, such as the above-described clocks. In this environment, the method of this invention is performed exclusively by the described self-actuating hardware, and comprises the non-mental steps of providing in the CPU 87 a first non-mental stored program hereinafter referred to as PPMTR, for providing communication between a first one of said PP's 81, e.g., PP 103, and said CPU for activating a second nonmental stored program, hereinafter referred to as AYN, in one of said PP's e.g., PP 103, said second nonmental stored program providing checks on the validity of the commands to and the validity of the responses from said one of said remote device, e.g., remote computer 25; and when said PP 103 becomes "hung-up" after the fact of a failure, e.g., in response to an invalid response from said device, then couples a second one of said PP's 81, e.g., PP 105, to said channel 77 and ac-

22

tivates a third non-mental stored program, hereinafter referred to as AIK, in PP 105, for restoring the functional ability of said PP 103; and providing in connection with said standard synchronizers and clocks, sequential time-based output information relating to the state of said device 25, whereby said computer system 21 retains its normal functional integrity independently of the functional integrity of said device 25. As will be understood in more detail hereinafter, the diagnostic of this invention also utilizes these same elements and programs to prevent failures before the fact in a failsafe manner, e.g., in the case of an invalid command function. Also, the method of this invention, treats the computer diagnostic process as another job without requiring dedication of the entire central processing unit i.e., CPU 87.

The synchronizers and clocks for the abovedescribed method and apparatus, comprise the abovementioned synchronizers which have suitable clocks, and couplers, which are illustrated in FIGS. 2 and 3 for operation with the mentioned stored programs to test channel 77, as illustrated in FIG. 4. To this end, the channel 77 is tested for function present, hereinafter referred to as FP. This involves the condition of the channel 77 to do certain activities, e.g., in connection with highly device dependent input and output activites, such as to set a conventional pick-up arm in disc 37, or to enlarge the size of the characters displayed by the CRT 71. Further tests, comprise the full/empty and active/inactive status of channel 77, hereinafter referred to as F/E and A/I. In this regard, these tests involve the directional F/E status of the channel 77 relative to whether the electrical condition thereof corresponds to bits from the CPU 87 to remote computer 25 or vice versa. Thus, for example, a directional full, i.e., predetermined bits (1) from the CPU to remote computer 25 is followed by a directional empty, i.e., predetermined bits (0), and this directional empty is followed by a directional full depending on whether the bits are transferred into CPU from computer or vice versa. The A/I status, refers to whether the channel 77 can receive or not. When active, the channel 77 is either full or empty, and when inactive is only empty.

As illustrated in FIGS. 4 and 5, a command bit or bit stream from PP 103 crosses channel 77 to a device, e.g., 6681 synchronizer 79, in the form of "data," a "data word," or as a "function" that propagates to the proper unit, e.g., remote computer 25, to produce a response in the form of a bit or bit stream. If the response returns to PP 103 as intended, there is no failure in the transmission from remote computer 25. If the response does not come back to PP 103, there has been a failure. Since the described hardware and the operation thereof with the correct non-mental software makes sure that the channel 77 is inactive prior to the issuance of the function, this assures when the function is issued that PP 103 will go to the next command. Then PP 103 waits for a reasonable length of time for an inactive signal, thus determining that the device accepted (i.e., recognized) the function, whereby the functions are issued sequentially periodically until there is a failure or error in the transmission in which case the failure is logged, and, depending on the gravity of the error, PP 105 comes in to substitute for PP 103, to remove the "hang-up," and to reactivate PP 103 to the next command sequence.

40

3,692,989

23   24

In accordance with this invention it is advantageous to provide the above-described diagnostic to de-bug the Brooknet system 21 without additional hang-ups in PP 81 and without destroying any data bits, bit streams, data words or command functions. This is particularly significant, since each and every PP 81 can undo what any other PP 81 can do. To this end, this invention provides a fail-safe non-mental software diagnostic, hereinafter referred to as Quest.

Quest is implemented as an independent non-mental subsystem, comprising a compiler 111, loader 113, and an execution monitor 115, which enable Quest to run in harmony with the above-mentioned CDC Scope operating system at the above described CSCF-11 and peripheral equipment 19, as described above and in more detail hereinafter.

To permit this as a non-mental job, a Fortran-like language is advantageously an integral part of Quest for enabling the user to write programs for execution in a portion of PP's 81 in such a manner that hardware failures from a device, and fatal software logic errors do not cause the PP's 81 to "hang-up," i.e., the user programs can be totally protected in relation to the system oration, thus enabling the user to run during actual production, as described above.

Basically, the Quest non-mental software, comprises three interacting non-mental programs, referred to above as PPMTR, AYN, and AIK, which in actual practice correspond for convenience to actual deck names for the system used in conjunction with Brooknet called Scope. The Quest hardware, comprises two basic elements. The elements are a central memory part 119, and PP parts, which comprise an AYN portion of PP 103 and an AIK portion of PP 105.

Each Quest job submitted by a user in the Quest language discussed in more detail hereinafter, is read, e.g., in CTR 71 one card at a time, which corresponds to a non-mental Quest command. If the card is not a command card, the card is copied verbatum to the output medium (i.e., printer 59 or 61), otherwise it is passed on to the macro compiler 121, referred to hereinafter as COMPI, which is in a portion of CPU 87 in CSCF 11. This COMPI generates the non-mental code associated therewith and builds up the variable and transfer tables corresponding thereto, which is a RAW CODE. When the last card is encountered, which is designated hereinafter as EOF, a preliminary error check is made. If there are no errors, control is passed to loader 113, which satisfies all variable and transfer references and packs the raw code to the PP code according to a fixed relocation scheme.

If no errors are detected and execution is desired, the initial call of arguments (40 PP words) are set up in the PP-CPU communications area and the generated code is appended to it (maximum is from 2,000 to 7,752, i.e., 5,752 PP words of code).

Control is then turned over to the driver monitor 125, hereinafter referred to as PPMTR, the PPMTR calls a pool PP e.g., PP 103 to load AYN, and as soon as AYN has accepted the arguments; it reads the generated code. Now both non-mental programs operate concurrently with PPMTR, directing and checking the activities of AYN. AYN must respond to the CPU 87 every 200B recalls (about 7 seconds, unless the timer command is used).

All AYN output messages are sent to the output file 127 and the central processor timer 129 of the PP (e.g., the PP-CPU timer of PP 103) is reset. However, there are AYN messages that are not sent to the output file 127, their sole purpose being to insure proper PP and CPU (i.e., PP 103 – CPU 87) communication.

Should AYN not respond in the allotted time interval, PPMTR calls a second PP, i.e., PP 105 and its stored non-mental program AIK to find out about the state of the AYN in PP 103. The AIK in PP 105 reports its findings to PPMTR who directs the latter either to recover AYN or to exit. This involves, (1) Quest routines and their interaction, (2) general flow, (3) flows and communications, comprising COMPI, LOADIT, AYN, and AIK, (4) sample program, (5) AYN resident routine index with timings, and (6) peripheral command flow timings

In an example of the AYN command index, the contents of CCI, a cell in AYN, corresponds to the following COMPILER MACROS: 0 argument check; 1 code check; 2 function; 3 inputs; 4 input; 5 inputn; 6 outputs; 7 output; 10 outputn; 11 sense; 12 compare; 13; 14 purge; 15 to go; 16 end; 17 call; 20 do; 21; 22 go; 23 print; 24; 25 finput; 26 ffinput; 45 argument error; 47 argument accept; 50 abort CPU 87; 51 begin pause; 52 end pause or end message; 53 print; 54 begin message; 55; 56 normal Quest termination; and 57 AYN active reply to CPU 87.

An example of the AIK command index, comprises: 60; 61 PP 103 is hung; 62 PP 103 is active; 63; 64 recovery terminated; 65 AIK is aborting due to an error; 66; 67.

An example of the PPMTR command index, comprises: 77 . . . 77xxxx; IF; xxxx = o abort; xxx = 1 - recover normally; xxx = 2 - abnormal recovery (DCN).

The Quest language for the described Brooknet computer system 21 involves, (1) a format of a Quest statement; (2) elements of Quest, comprising variables and constants; (3) the environment and program definition for Quest, comprising Quest, Select and Sub; and the Quest repertoire, comprising the following input/output (i.e., I/O) commands: (a) inputs, inputn, input, outputs, outputn, output, function, finput and ffinput; the following storage allocation: Dim; the following replacement statements: set, add, shift, index, store, and mask; and the following control statements: go to, go, do, term, call, return, end, sense, compare, purge, print, no print, msg, pause; the following deck organization: Example, the following printouts: dayfile messages and output format; and console control; and extensions.

Regarding the above-mentioned Extensions, the above described Quest I/O system illustrated in FIG. 7 was designed for a user with dedicated equipment with the user in control of selecting and deselecting the equipment. The channel could still be shared with an existing driver, but it was advantageous to provide fail-safe protection for the type of functions issued at execution. To this end, the user has two options: (a) he can execute in shared mode, in which case certain functions are inhibited from being issued (e.g., Master clear and mode 2 select) or (b) he can execute in non shared mode. In this mode no other user may share the channel for the duration of the test — but no functions are inhibited.

3,692,989

25

Since heretofore, if the proper "MAC" (Multiple access controller) switch was not deselected by the user it could deactivate the channel, this invention provides a select sequence to properly access the remote device with inherent fail-safety. To this end, therefore, this sequence deselects the 6681 synchronizer, selects the proper "MAC" switch and provides an input corresponding to the proper "MAC" switch status. If ready, control is given to the user. Otherwise, the deselect sequence gives up the channel or waits for a ready signal, i.e., a message to the console operator. The deselect sequence deselects the "MAC" switch 31 and gives up the channel, the synchronizer 6681 already being deselected. This permits the addition to the switch capability and the addition of further MACROS.

Also, this invention provides fail-safe accessing of CDC 3xxx equipment, illustrated in FIG. 1 as units of peripheral equipment, i.e., Peripheral Equipment, and illustrated in FIG. 2 as comprising discs, tapes and tape controllers, print controllers and printers, and displays. To this end, for the shared mode execution described as option A, the sequence provided, comprises: disable certain 6681 synchronizer functions (e.g., master clear and mode select); select/deselect the 6681 synchronizer; select/deselect the unit; and disable all but *o xxx* functions to the unit.

Some controllers can perform I/O functions on the unit after an N drop to the Quest job is given. Thereupon, the job drops and the PP exits. However, the unit is still actively performing the last I/O task whereupon the unit must be turned off, which can only happen in the protected mode on 3 xxx type equipment. Using the unprotected mode, this will not happen since the PP will master clear the channel prior to exiting.

Referring now in more detail to an actual example of one embodiment of the user documentation for the above-described diagnostic, referred to herein as the non-mental Quest software package, the following is a table of the "command index," the "AIK-command index," and the "CP command index:"

TABLE VII

COMMAND INDEX	ACTUAL COMMAND		
0	PAR. CHECK	26	FFINPUT
1	CODE. CHECK	50	MTRABT
2	FUNCTION	51	BEGIN PAUSE
3	INPUTS	52	END PAUSE
4	INPUT	53	PRINT
5	INPUTN	54	UNUSED
6	OUTPUTS	55	UNUSED E
7	OUTPUT	56	NORMAL TERMINATION
10	OUTPUTN	57	MESSAGE
11	SENSE		
12	COMPARE		
13			
14	PURGE		
15	GOTO		
16	END		
17	CALL		
20	DO		
21			
22	GO		
23	PRINT		
25	FINPUT		

	(AIK-COMMAND INDEX		
	UNUSED	60	
61	PP HUNG		
62	PP ACTIVE		
63	UNUSED		
64	RECOVERY TERMINATED		
65	UNUSED		

26

66	UNUSED
67	UNUSED
	(CP COMMAND INDEX)
70	ABORT PP
71	UNUSED
72	UNUSED
73	UNUSED
74	UNUSED
75	UNUSED
76	UNUSED
77	GO

In this example of the Quest software package, a compiler is required, which comprises three small Fortran-like language routines, i.e., TEST, ERROR, CODEP for I/O and an initial setup, two small compass routines (ISHIFT and DPFIX) for formating certain outputs and a large compass routine (COMPI) that does the actual compilation. COMPI comprises two main parts: a Command Processor (COMPI, ENTRY) and a Relocation Section (LOADIT, ENTRY).

Also, it will be understood from the following that a Command Processor (COMPI, ENTRY) is advantageously employed. This portion of the Quest software package, (1) decides on the function sought; and (2) processes this command to: (a) verify the arguments, (b) substitute the arguments into raw code, (c) initiate unsatisfied variable and transfer requests, and (d) store partially assembled code in a special array named CODE.

After the above described Quest software package is loaded from a permanent file on disk 37, initial environment parameters are obtained exclusively from the apparatus of CSCF 11 from a "user's program" card (such as the channel to be used, list and dump options, and whether or not execution is desired), as described in more detail hereinafter. In this regard, this card is located in the deck of cards corresponding to the "user's program" that is inserted into card reader 51. To this end also, as described in more detail hereinafter, information is punched into cards in the form of a "user's program" that is translated into a job, comprising binary electrical signals in the form of bits for storage on a disk, such as disk 37 and subsequent removal to CPU 87. Thus, when this "user's program" is scheduled by CSCF 11 as a regular job independently of the Quest software package, the "user's program" job is transferred automatically and exclusively by CPU 87 from the disk 37 to a portion of the central memory 119 of CPU 87.

Referring more particularly to the above-mentioned deck of "user's program" cards, this deck advantageously comprises a job card; the job card being the first card in the control card record, e.g., for use in connection with the CSCF 11, followed by control cards that tell the operating system, i.e., the CPU 87, the makeup of the "user's program" job as a regular job by CSCF 11. What follows are the Quest command cards. In this regard, this "user's program" has been transferred from the card reader 51 to the disc 37 and subsequently to a portion of the central memory 119 of the CPU 87 for operation in connection with the Quest software package when the system of CSCF 11 is ready to operate on this remote computer "user's program." As noted, however, the Quest software package job must also be requested by CPU 87 from the permanent file on disk 37 in accordance with the "user's program"

3,692,989

27

for the remote computer "user's program" job in CPU 87. The "user program" becomes input data for the Quest compiler. The quest compiler must reside in the CPU 87, and will process the user job "one card record " at a time.

[example]
Job card	User's program control
Control cards	record = control cards
EOR	

Quest Card	User's program = Command
Quest Commands	Cards
EOF	

1. The Job Card - Specifies the makeup of the job to the operating system, such as:
   How much core is required for the job
   How much time is required for the job
   How many print lines the job has
   Which billing account it is
   How many tapes the job uses
   How much ECS space is required

When the requested system resources become available, to the operating system it schedules the "-job" for execution.

2. The Control Cards — in the case of the Quest job, preforms the loading of the Quest subsystem as a job.

3. The Command Cards — are data cards to the Quest subsystem.
   a. Quest Card — specifies the "users" Equipment environment, i.e., which channel, execution, listing, etc.
   b. The remainder are the tasks to be performed.

To actuate the request for the described Quest software package, which request is made as a regular job by CPU 87, the remote computer "user's program" job control records are stored in CPU 87. Then the information stored therein continues to the control card in card reader 51 of this particular "user's program" job whereby CPU 87 brings into CPU 87 the described Quest software package from disk 37 where this permanent file is stored. This causes this Quest software package to be transferred from this permanent file of disk 37 into a portion of the memory of CPU 87. Thereupon, CPU 87 automatically processes the information in CPU 87 corresponding to next control card of the above-mentioned remote computer "user's program," which will be understood from the above to be the command to execute the Quest subsystem. Thus, this Quest subsystem is automatically executed exclusively by CPU 87 in connection with the described Quest software package that was transferred from the permanent file of disk 37 to a portion of the central memory 119 of the CPU 87.

The Quest subsystem now reads the "user's program" and processes it according to the user's specifications. The first "card" of the user's program must be the "Quest" card describing the user's execution environment. The remaining cards are the actual command cards, the last card in the user's program must be the end card.

In understanding this "user's program" job, it will be understood that the above-mentioned initial environment parameters are handled in the particular portion of the above-mentioned "user's program" of the

28

remote computer job that is transferred from card reader 51, to disk 37, to CPU 87 when the referred to job is scheduled by CSCF 11. The particular portion of the "user's program" for this remote computer job is referred to for convenience hereinafter as the Command Section thereof. When the "END" card of this "user's program" is detected, as described in more detail hereinafter, the Relocation Section of this "user's program" for this job is called.

As will be understood in more detail hereinafter, each word of the special array CODE of the Relocation Section contains a tag that indicates what type of action to take on that particular word before extracting the lower twelve bits as part of a final PP program, e.g., in PP 103 as described in more detail hereinafter in connection with the non-mental program AYN therein. In this regard, as also described hereinafter is more detail in connection with the INTERNAL MACRO STRUC-TURE, the loader LOADI: (1) allocates storage for all variables and arrays; (2) picks up the words from CODE and modifies them according to the above-mentioned tag to trigger such things as table look up for the absolute address of a variable, a request for an address relative to a present position, and other things necessary to link the code; and (3) extracts the lower 12 bits and packs them into full 60 bit words, whereby the code is ready for PP execution by PP 103 according to AYN if no errors occurred.

Relative to the above-mentioned MACRO STRUC-TURE, the following table illustrates one embodiment of an actual MACRO STRUCTURE:

TABLE VIII

INTERNAL MACRO STRUCTURE:
A 60 bit word is used:

CODE	MNEMONIC	ABS

CODE: The 12 bits are

TXXX

T=RELOCATION TYPE
XXX=THE OCTAL COUNT
T—CODES:

0	NO RELOCATION
1	CHANNEL SUBROUTINES
2	REL. FORWARD, XXX PLACES
3	REL. BACKWARD, XXX PLACES
4	ABSOLUTE XXX ENTRY
5	VARIABLE ALLOCATION
6	TRANSFER ALLOCATION
7	END OF CODE

RELOCATION TYPE 4 TABLE ENTRIES IN USE:
0	ILLEGAL	
1	MTRI	AYN MONITOR
2	MTR2	STATUS IN SHIFT ROUTINES
3	ERRACT	ERROR ACTIVE PROCESSOR
4	ERRINA	ERROR INACTIVE PROCESSOR
5	ERRFUL	ERROR FULL PROCESSOR
6	ERREMP	ERROR EMPTY PROCESSOR
7	ERRORS	COMPARE ERROR PROCESSOR
10	MTHABT	EXECUTION ABORT
11	PAUSE	ENTRY TO PAUSE
12	ERRXT	ERROR TRACE BACK
13	STATUS	LAST INPUT (MOST CURRENT STATUS)
14	ONE	CONSTANT 1
15	PRINT	PRINT ENTRY
16	MSG	MESSAGE ENTRY
17	TEMP	USER TEMPORARY
20	TEMP 1	USER TEMPORARY
21		OPEN
22		OPEN
21	FUNC	CHECK FUNCTION

From the above user documentation, it will be understood that Tables IX through XII represent actual operating sequences in the form of flow diagrams:

3,692,989

TABLE IX

Code	Name	Time (Major cycles)
OAM 73	Output (A) words fm m on channel d	4 plus 1/word

* = Memory Ref.

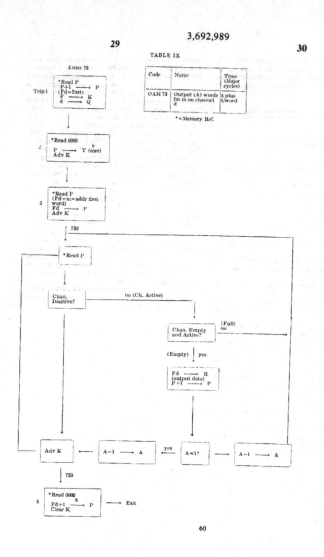

3,692,989

31 **32**

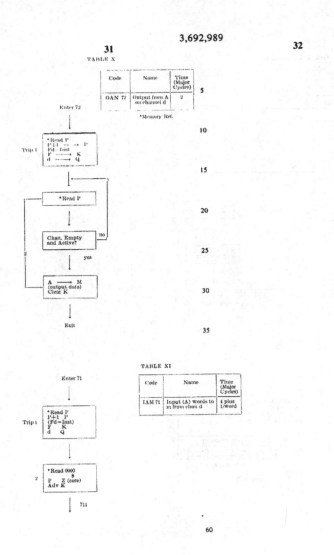

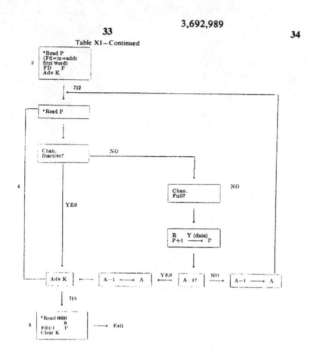

Table XI – Continued

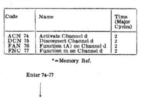

TABLE XII

Code	Name	Time (Major Cycles)
ACN 74	Activate Channel d	2
DCN 75	Disconnect Channel d	2
FAN 76	Function (A) on Channel d	2
FNC 77	Function m on Channel d	2

*= Memory Ref.

Enter 74-77

Table XII – Continued

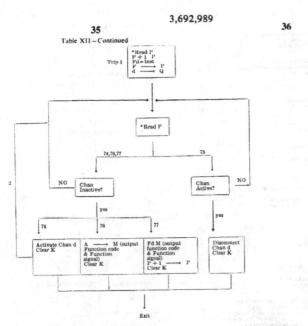

In regard to the above, the following Table XIII illustrates an actual AYN STRUCTURE for PP 103:

TABLE XIII

AYN STRUCTURE

LOC:	
1–77:	PERTINENT EXECUTION CELLS
1000–1775:	AVAILABLE SPACE FOR AYN RESIDENT
2000–7777:	AVAILABLE CORE FOR USER QUEST PROGRAM (DATA AND INSTRUCTIONS).
3000:	INITIALIZATION Area, gets overlayed by users program

NAMES & FUNCTION OF AYN RESIDENT ROUTINES:

SCPMES :	ISSUE INFORMATIVE MESSAGE TO CENTRAL
CPMES:	ISSUE INFORMATIVE MESSAGE TO CENTRAL
CRDABT:	READ ABORT FLAG, if set ABORT
PRINT:	ISSUE STANDARD Print message to CENTRAL
WATT:	WAIT FOR RESPONSE ON STANDARD MESSAGE: USES: CRDABT
ERRFUL:	SAVE (INDEX, "A", "P"), SET FULL STATE TIME ON FULL (4*64μs), if full does not arrive SET FATAL, PROCESS FATAL ERROR (ERRORF). If full arrives, check print, if 10 print, return.
ERRACT:	SAME AS ERRFUL BUT ON ACTIVE
ERRINA:	SAME AS ERRFUL, EXECT NO TIMING, ERROR IS ALWAYS FATAL
ERREMP:	SAME AS ERRFUL BUT ON EMPTY
ERRORS:	NOT FATAL ERROR (SENSE or Compare), NO TIMING, SAVES (INDEX,"A", "P") uses ERRORF.
MTR2:	PUSH DOWN STACK OF 5 STATUS

MTR1:	REGISTERS (INPUTS). ALL TRANSFER and I/O commands enter here
	1. Save command index and error transfer
	2. If previous command was fatal check restart, if set clear fatal, recover and continue. (ELSE EXIT)
	3. Check if it is time to communicate with the CPU (No Exit)
	4. Check if channel can be released
	a) No. Issue informative menage to CPU
	b) Yes. It current command an IO Yes exit. No. Go pause
	5. Reset CPU communications timer and exit
ERRORF:	All fatal errors enter here and are processed
FUNCC:	Protects function to be issued by user according to equipment and protection type
DESEL:	Deselects equipment
SELL:	Selects equipment
QFUNCv:	Issue function
INPUT:	Input equipment status
MSG:	Message Procedure
PAUSE:	Pause procedure
TRAC:	Track keeps count of the number of times the program is to be executed.
START:	Initialization
VERCH:	Modifies all Ch. references

Also, in this regard, the following Table XIV illustrates an actual AIK program for PP 105.

TABLE XIV

Recovery Driver (called by PPMTR)

AIK

3,692,989

37

AIK is called if AYN does not report back within
(≈6.4 sec of real time, 200₀ recalls). AIK
receives from Central, CH & BA.

CH = The channel AYN is using.
BA = PP-CP communications area (10 locs.)
i.e. absolute RA + BA

FUNCTION OF AIK:
1. Determine PP from channel
2. Check routine name at that PP and
   determine channel condition
3. Inform Central
4. Wait for reply
5. On positive reply (recovery), check
   channel, recover channel and exit

Channel criterion for recovery:
1. Channel must be reserved
2. AYN must be the offending routine
3. Channel is tested for 3 states:
   I: INACTNE
   II: ACTIVE & FULL
   III: ACTIVE & EMPTY
   The channel must stay in any one state for
   4*4096µs (≈16 ms)
4. On recovery response from Central test 3 is
   repeated—followed by recovery if necessary

RECOVERY:
	FOR:	ACTION:
I:	INACTIVE	ACN
II:	ACTIVE & FULL	IAN
III:	ACTIVE & EMPTY	OAN

Special recovery procedure:
  CENTRAL KEEPS TRACK OF THE
  RECOVERIES TAKEN
If the last 100 recoveries were of the same
state it initiates a special recovery
procedure.
  a) INACTIVE STATE:

ISSUED MESSAGE TO
OPERATOR TO
DISCONNECT HARDWARE.
(ACTIVATE FROM AIK IS
PREEMPTED BY
HARDWARE).
(JOB SHOULD BE
DROPPED)
Recovery is initiated

  b) ACTIVE STATE:

ISSUES MESSAGE TO
OPERATOR
(JOB SHOULD BE
DROPPED)
Direct AIK to recover
  with DCN
AIK waits for AYN to
  DROP
If AYN DROPS, AIK
  EXITS
If AYN does not DROP, informs
  central and recovery is
  initiated

AIK can be dropped anytime by typing
  0000 0000 0000 0000 7654 into its MSB+5
(Last word in MSB)

AIK does not respond to operator DROP, ONLY
ABORTS directed from Central or Manual
A typical PPMTR flow for CPU 87 is shown in Ta-
bles XV and XVI.

TABLE XV
PPMTR
|
SETUP AYN CALL
|

38

Table XV — Continued
CALL AYN
|
WAIT RESPONSE (Fixed Block)
|
ACCEPT
|
WAIT RESPONSE (CODE)
|
ACCEPT
|
Ⓐ
|

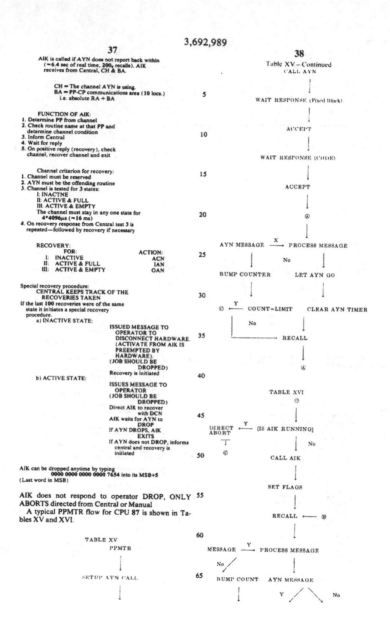

5
10
15
20
25
30
35
40
45
50
55
60
65

3,692,989

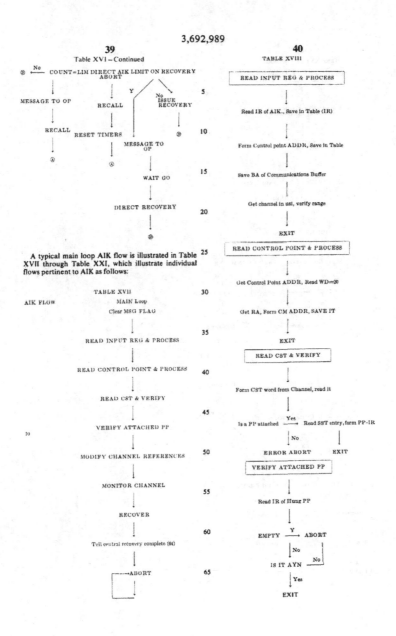

39

Table XVI – Continued

No
⑤ ← COUNT=LIM DIRECT AIK LIMIT ON RECOVERY
ABORT

MESSAGE TO OP

Y

No
ISSUE
RECOVERY   5

RECALL

RECALL   RESET TIMERS   ⑨   10

Ⓐ

MESSAGE TO
OP

Ⓐ

15
WAIT GO

DIRECT RECOVERY
20

⑤

A typical main loop AIK flow is illustrated in Table   25
XVII through Table XXI, which illustrate individual
flows pertinent to AIK as follows:

TABLE XVII   30
AIK FLOW   MAIN Loop
Clear MSG FLAG

35
READ INPUT REG & PROCESS

READ CONTROL POINT & PROCESS   40

READ CST & VERIFY
45

VERIFY ATTACHED PP

10

MODIFY CHANNEL REFERENCES   50

MONITOR CHANNEL
55

RECOVER
60

Tell central recovery complete (64)

←ABORT   65

40

TABLE XVIII

READ INPUT REG & PROCESS

Read IR of AIK., Save in Table (IR)

Form Control point ADDR, Save in Table

Save BA of Communications Buffer

Get channel in us1, verify range

EXIT

READ CONTROL POINT & PROCESS

Get Control Point ADDR, Read WD=20

Get RA, Form CM ADDR, SAVE IT

EXIT

READ CST & VERIFY

Form CST word from Channel, read it

Yes
Is a PP attached ——→ Read SST entry, form PP-IR

No

ERROR ABORT   EXIT

VERIFY ATTACHED PP

Read IR of Hung PP

Y
EMPTY ——→ ABORT

No

No
IS IT AYN ——

Yes

EXIT

49

41

3,692,989

42

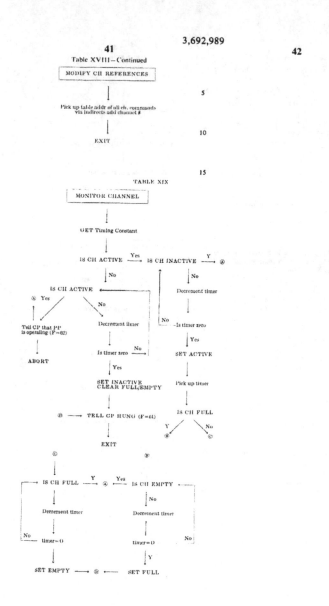

Table XVIII – Continued

MODIFY CH REFERENCES

Pick up table addr of all ch. commands
via indirects add channel #

EXIT

5

10

15

TABLE XIX

MONITOR CHANNEL

GET Timing Constant

3,692,989

43

TABLE XX

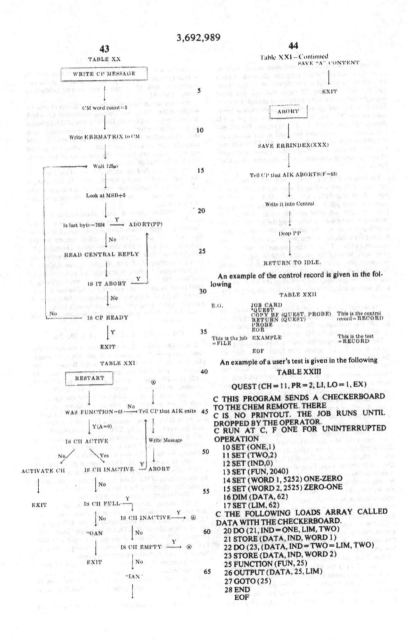

44

Table XXI—Continued

SAVE "A" CONTENT

EXIT

ABORT

SAVE ERRINDEX(XXX)

Tell CP that AIK ABORTS(F=65)

Write it into Central

Drop PP

RETURN TO IDLE.

An example of the control record is given in the following

TABLE XXII

E.G.   JOB CARD
        *QUEST
        COPY BF (QUEST, PROBE)   This is the control
        RETURN (QUEST)   record=RECORD
        PROBE
        EOF

This is the job EXAMPLE   This is the test
=FILE   =RECORD

        EOF

An example of a user's test is given in the following

TABLE XXIII

QUEST (CH = 11, PR = 2, LI, LO = 1, EX)

C THIS PROGRAM SENDS A CHECKERBOARD
TO THE CHEM REMOTE. THERE
C IS NO PRINTOUT. THE JOB RUNS UNTIL
DROPPED BY THE OPERATOR.
C RUN AT C, F ONE FOR UNINTERRUPTED
OPERATION

    10 SET (ONE,1)
    11 SET (TWO,2)
    12 SET (IND,0)
    13 SET (FUN, 2040)
    14 SET (WORD 1, 5252) ONE-ZERO
    15 SET (WORD 2, 2525) ZERO-ONE
    16 DIM (DATA, 62)
    17 SET (LIM, 62)
C THE FOLLOWING LOADS ARRAY CALLED
DATA WITH THE CHECKERBOARD.
    20 DO (21, IND = ONE, LIM, TWO)
    21 STORE (DATA, IND, WORD 1)
    22 DO (23, (DATA, IND = TWO = LIM, TWO)
    23 STORE (DATA, IND, WORD 2)
    25 FUNCTION (FUN, 25)
    26 OUTPUT (DATA, 25, LIM)
    27 GOTO (25)
    28 END
        EOF

3,692,989

45

46

In regard to the above-mentioned actual embodiment of this sample "user's program" the deck of cards corresponding thereto will be described. In this example, the deck contains 29 cards that are processed through card reader 51 by an operator skilled in the art. That is to say, the operator using conventional hardware causes the card reader 51 to process the cards through the card reader 51. In this regard, the pattern and location of the holes punched in the cards correspond to data for processing by CPU 87 in connection with the testing and diagnosis of remote computer 25 for the desired operation in the described Brooknet System 21.

The first card of the "user's program" is called the job card. This job card designates the beginning of a new Quest-diagnostic job for CSCF 11, which processes each job in sequence according to assigned priorities. This job card sets up initial environment parameters to be used in processing the job and for accounting purposes. The latter involves an account number for charging the machine usage to a particular account number. The other parameters, comprises priority, time limit of the job, the field length, i.e., the maximum amount of printer lines that will be used in the printer 59, and the user's name. These parameters are useful in queueing and executing the job in an orderly and meaningful way according to the proper priorities.

The second card is a control card that brings into the portion of the central memory 119 of CPU 87 from disk 37 the permanent file residing therein that corresponds to the described Quest software package.

The third card copies the Quest subsystem onto a file called Probe for Execution. The fourth card releases the file Quest (for other users). The fifth card directs the system to load the file Probe (which contains the Quest subsystem) and to execute it; (the sixth card indicates to the operating system the end of the control record for the users job). To this end, the execution involves the information from the other "user's program" cards. As will be understood in more detail hereinafter with reference to the "user's program" deck of this example, these other "user's program" cards, comprise cards seven through 29. The sixth card merely represents a record separator that designates the end of the control cards and the beginning of the "user's program," (EOR) which is data that is processed by the Quest software package. Like all the other cards, information corresponding to the card holes is stored in a portion of the memory of the CPU 87, but for ease of explanation, this stored information will be discussed with reference to actual "user's program" cards corresponding to the respective stored information derived from each respective "user's program" card.

Card seven called the Quest card, sets up the initial environmental parameters for the actual test run. In this regard, in this example, this run is designated to test the remote computer 25 to see if it behaves as desired. First the Quest software package is informed that channel 11 is the channel to be used to communicate with the remote computer 25. Other parameters, comprise "print option two." This option tells the Quest software package to write out the Quest error matrix on any fatal errors to the job's output file, which

resides on disk 37. Later, when the job output priority is high enough for printing, this information in the output file of disk 37 is transferred to and printed by printer 59 or 61.

Another actual option on this card seven in this example, is the "list option" having mnemonic LI, which is a binary type argument. The function of this option is to give a source listing of the PP code associated with the commands in the Quest "user's program," i.e., the cards in the deck of this example after the record separator card and before the last card of the deck, which is the "end of file" card, (EOF).

Another specified option on this actual card seven is the "loop option" having a mnemonic LO. This option functions to designate the number of times the entire "user's program" is to be executed. In this example, this is 1 time.

Still, another option on card seven, called the "execution option," functions to allow execution of the "user's program" when there are no logical errors in the "user's program." Other possible options for the cards in accordance with this invention, comprise a "dump option" that functions to point out exactly what is in the memory of PP–103. Another option, called the "restart option," whose mnemonic is RE, functions to continue the "user's program" upon encountering a fatal error. In an actual example that lacks this option, the whole job aborts upon encountering a fatal error. A sample "user's program" card seven with these additional latter above-mentioned options thereon would correspond to:

$$CH = 11, PR = 2, LI, LO = 1, EX, DU, RE$$

Card eight to card 29, comprise the remainder of the "user's program," and comment cards. Thus, for example, cards 8, 9, and 10, describe some feature of the "user's program" for the convenience of the user and cards 11 – 29 comprise an actual sample Quest "user's program" as illustrated heretofore in TABLE XXIII.

In operation, cards 11 – 29, except for the comment cards C, are accepted as data by the Quest software package now in a portion of the memory of CPU 87, and from this data the necessary PP code is automatically produced solely by CPU 87 to accomplish the testing of the remote computer 25. In this regard, this sample program generates an alternate bit pattern (i.e., a checkerboard) of 62 words and sends this pattern to the remote computer 25. Thereupon, if there are any fatal hardware errors the user will be informed thereof by the printing of the Quest error matrix on the user's output file which can be printed by printer 59 according to the print option as described above.

In this regard as shown in TABLE XXIII, certain constants are set up by the set commands of cards 10 – 15 and 17, such as are understood by one skilled in the art of conventional FORTRAN language. Thus, constants 1, 2, 0, 2,040 and 62 are set up for the user thus to accomplish the above-mentioned sending of the particular bit pattern to the remote computer.

The alternate bit patterns of cards 14 and 15 form the checkerboard by providing the necessary words, which are repeatedly stored (62 times) in the form of an alternate bit pattern in the array called DATA of card 16.

Cards 20 – 23 actually set up the above-mentioned

52

3,692,989

47

48

alternate bit pattern in a portion of the memory of PP 103, similarly to accomplishing a FORTRAN "do" operation a specified number of times (i.e. 62 times) and varying a constant in a specific way. In this case, the constant IND changes in value from 1 (i.e. ONE) to 62 (i.e. LIM) in steps of two (i.e. TWO). Stated another way, this would be equivalent to the progression 1, 3, 5, . . . 61.

The STORE command of card 21 sets every other word starting with card ONE of the array called DATA to the value 5252 (i.e., WORD 1). The next two cards 22 and 23 also form a "do" loop that does everything that the preceding two loop cards 20 and 21 did, except starting at word 2 i.e., the second word of the data array) and alternately sets every other word to the value 2525 (i.e. WORD 2). This, for example, is equivalent to the progression 2, 4, 6, . . . 62 to cover each position not covered by the preceding loop of cards 20 and 21.

Now that the desired checkerboard pattern is set into core (PP 103 memory), the hardware path must be established as well as readying the remote computer to receive the data. This is accomplished by the code associated with card No. 25. The function 2040, i.e., content of FUN, will be sent over the channel. Each digit of this function has special meaning to the hardware as follows:

```
2    Synchronizer address
0    RCA address
4    Function desired (in this case 4 =
                        Write data)
0    LCU address
```

When the above-mentioned function is received properly by the hardware, the data path is established and the remote computer 25 is ready to receive the data (checkerboard). If, for some reason, an error occurs on this step, the QUEST user will be informed and the function will be issued again. Note that the second argument of card No. 25 is the error transfer and in this case it is back to itself (statement number 25).

The next step is to actually output the data (checkerboard). This is accomplished by the code associated with card No. 26. There will be 62 (LIM) words output from the array called DATA and if a hardware error occurs on this transmission, control will be passed to the code associated with card No. 25 (statement number 25).

The code associated with card 27 will pass control to the beginning of the function—output sequence thus repeating the process indefinitely.

The code associated with card No. 28 marks the logical end of the QUEST user's program. If control is ever passed to this code, the job will abort or repeat depending on the above-mentioned loop option (LO).

Card No. 29 is an end-of-file indicator. It informs the 6600 operating system that this is the logical end of this job.

While the above has described one embodiment of this invention, involving the described MACRO, it will be understood that this invention also contemplates another embodiment, comprising a procedure for adding new (or additional) MACROS. The method of this embodiment is illustrated as follows in TABLE XXIV:

PROCEDURE FOR ADDING NEW MACROS

I. General steps

1. Insert the name of the macro at the end of the "available functions" table (AVFN) in right justified display code.
2. Insert a jump to the section that will process the macro at the end of the PHASE 3 section (Table OP). The format of this is as follows:

TABLE XX   JP   PF XX

Note: XX will be used to denote a two
      digit number.

3. Insert the actual macro processor (see section II) with a PFXX (from step 2) as its entry name. Each "processor" section will depend on the particular action needed by that particular macro, but all have some common properties and restrictions:
   a. Address register A1 contains the address minus one of the table that contains the macro arguments in order (ARGA). (At this point these arguments are in display code).
   b After "processing," address register A1 must be set to the address of the first word of the raw code and a return jump to CSTOR executed. This will transfer the raw code to a special buffer and list the mnemonics if called for.
4 Insert the actual raw code macro in the data section of COMPI. Each word of this macro must conform to the following format:

12 bits	36 bits		12 bits
RELOCATION	MNEMONIC OF	ACTUAL PP	ACTUAL PP
	INSTRUCTION IN LEFT	INSTRUCTION	INSTRUCTION
	JUSTIFICATION DIS	PLAY	
DIRECTIVE	CODE		IN OCTAL

Indirect addressing is used for channel modification and inserting arguments into the raw code.

II. Macro processor tasks

1 Insert argument names (ARGA), transfer names and relocation directives into raw code.
   a. Put address labels in proper place in raw code.
   b. Insert entrys into indirect address table (ZZXX) using VFD 60/NNNNN where NNNNN is the label used in (a).
   c. Set address register A3 equal to the address of the first word of this entry (step b) and do successive return jumps to PVAR, PVARF, or PTR for variable, required variable or transfer table look-ups respectively. These three routines will cause the name of the variable or transfer to be put in the raw code as well as the proper relocation directive.
   d. If any macro arguments are the "not required" type, they must be set to their forfeit values initially in the raw code.
   This means they must be restored after the call to CSTOR to allow further use of the raw code.
   e. The final instruction in the macro processor is unconditional jump to COMPI.
   Note: all macros requiring channel modifications must do the following:
   a. Put address labels in the proper place in the raw code
   b. Insert an entry into the T XX table using VFD 60/CHXX where CHXX is the address label from (a).

3,692,989

49

NOTE

CHANGES TO AYN RESIDENT

When changes to the resident are necessary the following tables must match in content and order.

1 IN"COMPI" = PPTB (COMPI. 2456)
2 IN"AYN" = (JTAB (AYN. 7/5)

This invention has the advantage of providing computer apparatus for self-diagnosis of both hardware and software errors and/or malfunctions as a regular computer job without interrupting the operation of the computer for any of a plurality of other regular computer jobs. In one embodiment, this invention forms a shared-time computer system having diagnostic means for connecting with a central computer, innumerable new, complicated and/or experimental input – output devices, such as a plurality of remote computers, in an efficient, time-saving manner. In this regard, this invention has the advantage of providing an improved diagnostic for the Brooknet shared-time computer system at the Brookhaven National Laboratory, comprising improved hardware and a novel non-mental software package, called Quest. To this end, the invention has the particular advantage of operating and diagnosing computer hardware and non-mental software in central and remote locations by means of central diagnostic hardware, comprising a portion of the central memory of a specific central processing unit having two peripheral processors forming small computer control units for each other and the central processing unit. Also, a specific diagnostic, comprising a unique Quest software package is provided having three specific non-mental programs for operation exclusively by a central shared-time computer system.

What is claimed is:

1. A time-sharing computer system having central and remote input - output means, comprising a central scientific computer facility having central processing means forming a central memory and means for performing various arithmetical and logical operations, and a plurality of peripheral processor means for providing small computer control units for said central processing means with equal power to provide and destroy information and commands for execution in each of said peripheral processor means and said central processing means with said remote input - output means for communications therebetween on a regular, time-sharing job basis, said remote input - output devices, comprising at least one computer for connection to said central processing means on a regular, time-sharing job basis by said peripheral processor means, and at least two of said peripheral processor means forming with a portion of said memory a diagnostic means for diagnosing errors and malfunctions in said communications between said central processing means and said remote input - output means for preventing malfunctions in said peripheral processor means exclusively by said central scientific computer facility as a regular job without dedicating said central scientific computer facility to said diagnostic means for quickly and efficiently connecting said central processing means and said remote input - output means or quickly and efficiently providing said time-sharing computer system for providing said communications

50

between said central and remote input - output means for trouble-free operation.

2. Method of testing and diagnosing the communication and failures of communication between a computer and an input - output means, comprising the active on-line steps of:

a. selectively transmitting information between said means and said computer as a first job by means of a first portion of said computer without dedicating the entire computer to said first job; and

b. recording said selective transmission and said failures of said transmission as part of said first job by means of said first portion of said computer without dedicating the entire computer to said first job; said computer again selectively the dedication of

c. said first portion of said computer being responsive to said failures for activating a second portion of said computer as a part of said first job for removing said failure without dedicating the entire computer to said first job whereby said first portion of said computer again selectively transmits said information without the dedication of the entire computer to said first job.

3. Method of diagnosing and testing the communication between any device, for generating or receiving input and/or output signals and a computer comprising the active on-line steps of:

a. selectively transmitting information between said device and said computer through a portion of said computer; and

b. recording said transmissions including failures thereof by means of said portion of said computer;

c. said portion of said computer being responsive to said failure for activating another portion of said computer for removing said failure whereby said first portion of said computer again continues said selective transmission of said information without dedicating the entire computer to any of these tasks.

4. The invention of claim 3 in which said failure removal is controlled by said first portion of said computer for the repetition and termination of said method in a predetermined time.

5. Method of testing the transmissions to and from a computer for diagnosing the failures of communications to and from the computer and another device, such as a remote signal generating and receiving means, comprising the active on-line steps of:

a. continuously employing a first portion of said computer to the first task of selectively transmitting said communications between said device and said computer without dedicating the entire computer to said first task;

b. continuously employing said first portion of said computer to the second task of recording said transmissions without dedicating the entire computer to said second task;

c. continuously employing said first portion of said computer to the third task of recording said failures of communications without dedicating the entire computer to said third task; and

d. continuously employing said first portion of said computer to the fourth task of activating a second portion of said computer for identifying said failures of said communications without dedicat-

3,692,989

51

ing the entire computer to said fourth task; said first portion of said computer being responsive to said recording of said failures of said communications for repeatedly activating said second portion of said computer for repeating said task for removing the same without dedicating the entire computer thereto.

6. Method of operating a computer until a blockage develops, and then reducing the blockage in an orderly manner for determining what the blockage was and where it was located without tying up the whole computer, said computer having a central processor, a plurality of peripheral processors, and a plurality of data channels connected thereto, comprising the active on-line step of selectively connecting said central processor with at least one of said peripheral processors and a signal generating station by monitoring means responsive to a program for monitoring the peripheral processors, said monitoring means being responsive to an invalid response from said signal generating station for selectively connecting said central processor with another peripheral processor for removing said invalid response.

7. The invention of claim 6 in which said second peripheral processor dumps the information in said first peripheral processor in an orderly manner while logging the same for locating the source of said invalid response.

8. Data processing system, consisting of central processing means having a central processing unit and peripheral processing means for communicating with a plurality of remote input - output means for exclusively, automatically, and non-mentally scheduling and simultaneously self-operating a plurality of regular computer jobs, comprising the diagnosis of failures in the communication between at least one of said peripheral processing means, said central processing unit and one of said remote input - output means while said central processing unit, other of said peripheral processing means, and other of said remote input - output means are in communication for the performance of other regular computer jobs.

9. In a central computer connected to a remote input - output device that is coupled to at least one of a plurality of data channels for communication of binary, electrical, input - output signals between said central

52

computer and said remote device, said central computer having a central processor and peripheral processors for controlling the communication of said binary, electrical, input - output signals in the form of commands and responses between said central processor and said remote input - output device by selectively coupling at least one of said data channels between at least one of said peripheral processors and said central processor, said one of said peripheral processors becoming inoperative to perform its control function for said communication in response to an invalid response from said remote input - output device, the method of analyzing the functional integrity of said plurality of data channels, comprising the step of providing for said central processor a first, stored, non-mental program that monitors the state of said first one of said peripheral processors coupled to said data channels, activates a second, stored, non-mental program in said first one of said peripheral processors, for providing checks on the validity of the commands to the remote input - output device and also the validity of the responses of said remote input –output device, and when said first of said peripheral processors becomes inoperative in response to an invalid response from said remote input - output device then couples a second one of said peripheral processes to said one of said plurality of data channels and activates a third, stored, non-mental program in said second one of said peripheral processors for restoring the functional ability of said first one of said peripheral processors, to couple said central processor across said one of said data channels to said remote input - output device for the communication of said commands and response therebetween, whereby said central computer retains its normal functional integrity independent of the functional integrity of said remote input - output device.

10. The method of claim 9, comprising the step of effecting time based checks on the validity of the responses of said remote input - output device in accordance with the state of said remote input - output device for providing sequential time-based output information on the state of said remote input - output device.

* * * * *

50

55

60

65

55

Epilogue

When I left TELSTAT all my products were in tip top shape. ASSIST would get us into the door of every Financial Company, Bank, Brokerage House and Insurance Company, and allow our salesmen to sell the consolidated products and the Rational Corporate Bond Model. At that time Telstat "OWNED" the "Financial Industry."

Wall Street however does not let you sit idly by on your laurels. Thus, pretty soon many pricing services sprung up for Corporate Bonds and began competing with TELSTAT's products. They were not pricing models but "GURU DRIVEN ESTIMATES of CORPORATE PRICES." Large Brokerage Houses entered the field such as MERRYL LYNCH and others. Of course they could not offer the broad variety of services my Corporate Bond Model provided. That is, no dynamic Quality Ratings and so on.

However, while ASSIST was static, that is, it was not affected by market conditions, the Rational Corporate Bond Model was not. As market yields changed drastically the model needed to have the boundary conditions changed. Penny assigned a programmer, but he could do nothing. He just did not understand the underlying mathematics and the effect of the boundary conditions.

Thus, the model started to produce absurd prices or no prices at all. All this happened at the time when Telstat reached the final stages of acquisition by Western Union.

So, PENNY embarked on a program to squeeze out every dollar she could out of the products she had. She decided to sell ASSIST on an "as is" basis. Rumors had it, I was told by some insiders, that she sold over 5 copies of ASSIST at $250,000 each. However, as it turned out none of the copies worked properly because nobody had the same operating system as Telstat. Telstat's system had a "TREE LOADER" which was unlike

57

anything in the market, especially for IBM products. The upshot was that Telstat was acquired by Western Union at $24.00 a share.

I should mention that Wall Street operates mostly on "SOFT DOLLARS." The trick is to covert soft dollars into hard dollars. First, let's define "SOFT DOLLARS."

Every portfolio manager trades either stocks or bonds in the course of a month. Each time he trades he pays a commission. And, every brokerage house wants to get these commission dollars. Since the trades are relatively large, often in the million dollar range, many brokers are willing to pay back in "SOFT DOLLARS." That is, the trader accrues "SOFT DOLLARS," which he can apply to any "BUSINESS RELATED EXPENSE." Such as: Transportation, Entertainment, Pricing Services, Portfolio Services and much more.

Thus, portfolio managers have a huge amount of "potentially" ready cash waiting to be used. Therefore, when you sell a financial service, you have to be prepared to have your own broker who gives you the maximum soft dollars, converted to hard dollars. As you can see, portfolio managers are highly sought after individuals when it comes to tap their "SOFT DOLLAR RESOURCES."

When Penny sold her stock in Telstat, she ended up being the largest shareholder in Western Union. Bill Stern and Penny supported MARIO CUOMO and BESS MYERSEN. Since their contributions were sizable, Bill Stern became COMMISSIONER in NEW YORK CITY.

The situation at BROOKHAVEN LABS was totally different. There, I had a maintenance contract and when even the slightest problem arose, I was called in to fix it or provided an alternate solution. In this way the Patent Software was running smoothly both at Brookhaven and at Control Data. (I am sure Yosh had a side deal with Control Data).

While I did not get a Nobel Prize, I was always prominently featured as the crowning achievement of APPLIED MATH. In fact, in the brochure featuring Brookhaven's 50 year existence, my Patent was the feature achievement of the Applied Mathematics Department throughout their existence.

In Control Data, my Patent was applauded a different way. Some times later, CONTROL DATA developed a new Operating System called KRONOS. In that operating system, my software became an integral part as a channel recovery system.

In addition, the US Government sold the rights to my Patent to a company called TANDEM. They built computers using my "FAIL SAFETY" method. (I got all the credits but the US GOVERNMENT owned my patent, since I worked at Brookhaven and we were paid by a Government Agency).

Most importantly my Patent opened up a whole new era of software development. New software could be patented using my methodology.

Many years later, in 1980, I started my own consulting business. Telstat was now under new management from Western Union and they were totally clue less as to how my products functioned. When they found out that I was available as a consultant, they offered me a very nice consultant contract for ASSIST and CBM.

Assist worked perfectly, so it required no maintenance at all. But, the Corporate Bond Model needed extensive work, primarily to accommodate the new "YIELD MARKET."

When I originally developed the model, Coupon rates varied from 2 to 10 percent. By 1980, rates had increased to 15% for the Bellwether bond, and 24% for the BAA Corporates. In addition, the qualities AA, A and BAA were subdivided into 1, 2, 3 subsets. In fact the claim was made that there were no AAA Corporate Bonds. Also, a new form of Bond became very popular. Every brokerage house called them by a different name and became known as the WALL STREET ZOO (CATS, DOGS etc.).

Essentially they were GOVERNMENT BONDS where the COUPON was "Stripped." Thus the Brokerage house kept the Coupon, while the remainder was sold as a ZERO COUPON BOND.

Thus, the YIELD SURFACES took on a whole new shape, ranging from ZERO to MAXIMUM Coupon, requiring a whole lot more data than before. This is when my "MODEL LIBRARY" paid handsome dividends.

In addition, Michael Milken was in jail and it became extremely difficult to get trade data for JUNK BONDS

When all that was completed, the next major phase was to bring back the many clients Telstat lost when the model did not perform properly.

A new major competitor arrived on the scene: ITSI. ITSI was owned by Chase Manhattan Bank and they had developed a GURU based model which used the PORTFOLIO of Chase for their underlying model. However, the YIELD MARKET had peeked by 1980 and yields began to decline. This played havoc in the GURU based models but were a shoe in my model (Call Schedules).

The Telstat Database included all the elements needed to compute the call schedule: Starting date, Ending date and starting CALL PREMIUM. This way the CURRENT DATE to the STARTING DATE was the call protection period. The STARTING DATE and the CALL PRICE was the beginning of the CALL PERIOD and AMOUNT and the Ending had an implied amount of ZERO call premium. Thus, the entire call schedule could be developed and "superimposed" on the model price to yield the market price. Only then is the MARKET PRICE converted to a MARKET YIELD.

Once the model was working properly, Telstat started to get most clients back. But, at that time WESTERN UNION lost a satellite in space (a 100 million dollar gizmo). And, as money was tight, the major bank of WESTERN UNION wanted payment on the lost satellite. So, WESTERN UNION started to sell some of the divisions they had acquired and that included TELSTAT.

Solomon Brothers got the call by Western Union to sell TELSTAT. The going price was 6 million dollars. I found an investor who was willing to buy Telstat and we entered a bid of 6 million dollars. But, we found out that TELSTAT was sold to CHASE. (Apparently, Chase wanted Telstat's client base for ITSI which CHASE owned. In fact WESTERN UNION was told that if CHASE does not get TELSTAT, they would cancel WESTERN UNIONS credit line). Goes to show you. There is no "fair play" in big business.

I had a lawyer who urged me to sue CHASE, WESTERN UNION and TELSTAT. Unfortunately I don't have the funds for such a venture. So, right or wrong, I passed it up.

Printed in the United States
By Bookmasters